COOL
CHARACTERS
with
SWEATY
PALMS

COOL CHARACTERS *with* SWEATY PALMS

MARK R. LITTLETON

VICTOR BOOKS®

A DIVISION OF SCRIPTURE PRESS PUBLICATIONS INC.
USA CANADA ENGLAND

COOL CHARACTERS WITH SWEATY PALMS is a
study of how different Bible characters handled trying situations. It stresses that the same principles are applicable
for believers today. Student activity booklets (Rip-Off
Sheets) and a leader's guide with visual aids (SonPower
Multiuse Transparency Masters) are available from your local
Christian bookstore or from the publisher.

Scripture taken from the *Holy Bible, New International
Version,* © 1973, 1978, 1984, International Bible Society.
Used by permission of Zondervan Bible Publishers. Other
Scripture quotations are from *New American Standard Bible*
(NASB), © the Lockman Foundation 1960, 1962, 1963,
1968, 1971, 1972, 1973, 1975, 1977.

Library of Congress Catalog Card Number: 88-62830

ISBN: 0-89693-639-2

Recommended Dewey Decimal Classification: 248.83
Suggested Subject Heading: YOUTH—RELIGIOUS LIFE

TABLE OF CONTENTS

To the many young people
who ministered to me
when the days were tough
and the nights were long

The evangelistic team of Boardwalk Chapel
Wildwood, New Jersey
Summer 1973, 1974

The youth group and leaders of
The Evangelical Free Church of Hershey
Hershey, Pennsylvania
Summer 1975

The singles group of Fellowship Bible Church
Richardson, Texas
1974–1978

The youth group of Englewood Christian Church
Indianapolis, Indiana
1978–1980

The youth group of Berea Baptist Church
Glen Burnie, Maryland
1980–1984

INTRODUCTION

Do you tend to think of biblical characters as spiritual "giants," people who faced incredible circumstances, yet always triumphed, walked victoriously with Jesus, and ended up in Hebrews 11 as members of the "Faith Hall of Fame"? You may be in for a surprise. Some of those "revered heroes" sweated it out in the trenches just like us. They had doubts, fears, and second thoughts too. As a matter of fact, most Bible characters were just like you and me. That's why we can learn so much from them.

There are a lot of circumstances that make me uncomfortable—things like confronting someone who has committed a sin (especially if he or she is bigger and more important than me); or having to help someone when it's highly inconvenient; or standing up for my convictions even when everyone else in the room says it's all right not to.

How do you do it? How do you stand up in those times?

That's what this book is about. I hope it will help you face many of the common, everyday experiences that have an uncanny ability to hurt us for life if we're not careful. We'll look at fifteen biblical people thrust into perilous but common situations, and see what they did. The steps they took can help us in facing our own circumstances.

At the start, though, I'd like to make you aware of several important principles on which this book is built.

First, the Bible was written to encourage us. Read Romans 15:4: "For everything that was written in the past was written to teach us, so that through endurance and the encouragement of the Scriptures we might have hope."

That's quite an incredible statement. Look at what it reveals:

1. The Bible was written to teach us. Paul was referring to a special kind of teaching—the teaching of facts and principles. Few of us have the discipline and insight to learn on our own. We must be taught. What we must be taught are facts and principles, especially those recorded in Scripture. One of the primary purposes of the Bible is to gather all those facts and principles in one place.

2. The Bible was written to give us hope. Hope is the expectation and confidence that certain things will happen in the future. What is it that Christians hope will happen? That Jesus will come back for us, and take us to His kingdom where we'll reign with Him forever; that He will transform us from being sinners to being perfect pictures of Himself in character and person; and that all the evil of this world will be disposed of once and for all. These hopes fuel us, inspire us, keep us moving forward. Without them, this world would be little more than a glorified graveyard.

3. The Bible stresses perseverance and encouragement. Perseverance is our part. It involves "hanging

in there," giving it our all, and continuing to strive and move forward, knowing nothing will stop us. Perseverance is determining to see the job through.

Encouragement could also be translated "consolation" or "comfort." That comes from above. It's assurance and reassurance. It's the still, small voice telling us that Scripture is all true and that God will bring us to glory.

The Bible was written for these reasons. It's meant to be a source of encouragement, not condemnation. It's meant to heal us with grace, not handicap us with guilt.

A second principle on which this book is based is that Christians have problems. In fact, they often have more problems than non-Christians. Did you catch that? Here it is again. "Christians have problems. In fact, they often have more problems than non-Christians."

"Come on!" you may be saying. "We're supposed to be living the victorious life! We're supposed to be triumphant!"

Of course we are. But we're also doing battle on the front lines of God's kingdom. That means struggles, temptations, and rejection. Believe me, anyone who's living for Jesus Christ is Satan's enemy. Why? Because that person is fighting the only battle that matters and Satan wants it stopped.

Look at it this way. If Satan has a person safely caught up in a cult, or another religion, or atheism, why should he attack them? In fact, he should make it easier on that person so he'll feel secure. That will keep them safely locked in a "holding cell" until death.

But for the Christian it's a different story. A Christian could lead someone else to Christ. He could tell others the truth. His life could catch the eye of some lost person and arouse interest. So Satan pulls out all the stops. He attacks with every flaming missile he has. He wants to make the Christian speak bad, act bad, and look bad—anything to neutralize him.

So you should expect that you may tangle with more problems, and deeper problems, than any of your non-Christian friends. In fact, it might be helpful to memorize a verse in 1 Peter about it: "If you are insulted because of the name of Christ, you are blessed, for the Spirit of glory and of God rests on you" (1 Peter 4:14). Problems are a sign that the "Spirit of glory and of God rests on you."

Now don't get me wrong. Some problems are caused by our sins and mistakes. That's a different story. But if you're walking with Jesus and seeking to obey Him, and problems pop up, rejoice. You're blessed.

Third, I want to stress that God *wants* us to face problems. The thing to do with problems is not to run from them, deny them, repress them, or pretend they don't exist. It's to confront them head-on.

This book takes fifteen characters and shows you their desperate situations. From them we discover the principles that helped them triumph (and in some cases, the principles which would have helped them, but which they failed to apply).

Remember when Jesus told the disciples that they'd all deny Him at the crucifixion? What happened? All of them swore they'd never do such a thing—Peter, most of all. Then Jesus told Peter not only would he deny Him, but he'd do it three times that very night!

Peter was adamant. "No way will I ever deny you," was his basic response. But Jesus warned him that Satan would "sift him like wheat." Jesus was trying to get Peter to face the problem—his cowardice, his lack of boldness, his weakness in the face of death. Had Peter faced it and admitted it, he might never have denied Jesus at all.

My plan in this book is to demonstrate the four steps to problem-solving:

1. Admit that you have problems. Simply confess them.

2. Define your problems specifically. Without knowing them, you can't fight them.

3. See that the answer to your problems is Scripture.

4. Apply scriptural principles to your problems.

Are you willing to do that? If not, stop reading. There's no point in continuing on. This book isn't meant to entertain you; it's meant to transform you under the Spirit's directives.

Fourth, I'd like you to realize that many problems do not have instant solutions. As you get into this book, you're going to find people who wrestled for years with certain problems. They couldn't just click their heels three times and have the problem disappear. They had a long, hard fight. Jesus never said, "I came to give you three-minute solutions to your problems."

Can you accept that? Our world, especially the media, has made us think that anything can be solved in thirty minutes (the average length for a TV show). If it can't be dealt with in that time, don't try to deal with it. Even the most intense problems—abortion, child abuse, murder, rape—are all solved within two-hour TV movies. Luke Skywalker solved all the problems of the universe in less than six hours of movie time!

But anyone who seeks to walk with Christ is in it for life. You'll face hordes of problems as a Christian, but they're all designed to strengthen and build you, to make you a little more like Jesus. So prepare yourself for long-distance running. This isn't a hundred-yard dash we're in. This is the marathon.

Fifth, I want to make it clear that God promises to go with us through every problem we face. "I will be with you always, to the very end of the age" (Matthew 28:20). "So do not fear, for I am with you; do not be dismayed, for I am your God. I will strengthen you and help you; I will uphold you with My righteous right hand" (Isaiah 41:10). "The Lord is my helper; I will not be afraid. What can man do to me?" (Hebrews 13:6)

The great truth of Christianity is this: you're not in this struggle alone; the God of Creation, the Lord of the universe, the One who made you, me, and everyone else dwells right inside each of His people.

That's a tremendous truth, isn't it? God with us. God in us. God around us. God ahead, behind, over, and under us. God everywhere. We can't go anywhere without Him already being there. He has already paved the way, and has already planned our success. For we are God's workmanship, created in Christ Jesus to do good works, which God prepared in advance for us to do (Ephesians 2:10). There is no reason ever to fear again. The Lord of Creation is with us.

It's important that I make you aware of one more thing before you begin. Each one of the following chapters begins with a dramatized—*fictionalized*—Bible story. In the dramatizations, I've tried to provide a glimpse into the minds and hearts of some of God's greatest saints. I've taken some liberties with some of the stories, and you may find yourself disagreeing with my fictionalization. That's fine. I would strongly encourage you to read the actual passages in the Bible and create your own scenarios of what these saints were like.

What's important is that we identify with these people. Joseph, Moses, Mary, and all the others struggled just like us. It's my hope that as you travel the "highway of holiness," you'll find the going a little smoother because of what you learned from biblical people who walked the same road.

1

SHADRACH, MESHACH, AND ABEDNEGO

INTO THE FURNACE

Shadrach stared dismally out the window onto the plain of Dura. *The idol is going up fast,* he thought. *The dedication will happen in less than a week.*

His thoughts turned again to the king's decree. Every official in the kingdom had been commanded to attend the dedication. But why? To worship the idol? What did the king want? Did it have anything to do with the dream Daniel had interpreted?

He shifted uneasily and glanced at Abednego who was reading on the sofa. *He never gets upset about anything,* Shadrach thought. *Sometimes I wish I could be like that.*

He looked again at the idol. Perhaps it did have something to do with the dream. (The king had seen a monstrous statue with a head of gold, chest of silver, belly and thighs of bronze, legs of iron, and feet of iron and clay. Daniel told him that the golden head symbolized Nebuchadnezzar himself, and that his kingdom would perish and give way to a second, the silver. The king wasn't pleased to hear that, but he did promote Daniel for interpreting the dream.)

Suddenly Shadrach saw its meaning. "It's an oath of loyalty," he said to Abednego.

Abednego looked up. "An oath of loyalty?"

"Yes," said Shadrach. He began to pace. "The king is trying to make sure that his kingdom doesn't fall. He's planning to use this idol to sift out any traitors, anyone who's not absolutely loyal to him."

"Huh!" Abednego said with a snort. "I'll be loyal to him, but I won't worship the idol. It's against God's Law."

Shadrach looked away. "That's the problem. If we don't worship the idol, we'll be thrown into the furnace. I'm sure that's it. That's why he's building the furnace next to it—to make the loyalty oath that much more compelling. We're doomed."

Abednego shook his head. "Oh, come on. Jehovah will protect us."

Shadrach thought for a moment, then said, "Maybe we don't have to stop worshiping Jehovah. Maybe we could just bow to the image and be done with it."

"You think it's that easy—just fall down for a moment and worship an idol?" said Abednego. "What about the Law? Are you willing to disobey the Law?"

"Well, it wouldn't be disobeying. We'd just be trying to . . . preserve life."

Abednego snorted. "You know we can't look at it that way. Jehovah is testing us. We have to obey Him. I for one won't worship the idol."

Shadrach glanced at Abednego. "You're right. We'll both refuse to worship the idol and accept whatever happens. Pact?"

Abednego smiled. "Pact."

The two men joined hands and prayed. Later, when Meshach came by, he agreed with them. No matter what happened, the three of them wouldn't worship the idol.

Two weeks later, the day of the dedication arrived. Sublime music and majestic speeches filled the air. The image glimmered in the sunlight. The people had to shield their eyes to behold it. Next to it was the monstrous kiln furnace. Smoke and flames erupted continuously from the huge hole in the top.

Shadrach, Meshach, and Abednego stood on the back part of the platform, concealed by the splendid uniforms of Nebuchadnezzar's highest officials.

A herald stood before the crowd with a trumpet in his hands. Nebuchadnezzar rose. His gravelly voice rang out over the platform. "To you the command is given, O people. At the moment you hear the sound of the music, you will fall down and worship the golden image. Whoever doesn't worship will immediately be cast into the midst of the furnace of blazing fire." He motioned to the furnace to the right of the image.

The herald placed the trumpet to his lips. The blast on it jolted the orchestra into action. A sweet, beautiful music filled the air and the gathered officials fell forward on their faces. The king himself was the first to fall.

But far in the back, Shadrach and his two friends stood erect, unwilling to break the commandment of their God.

When the music finished a small group rushed to the king. Nardi, a chief advisor, seethed, "They didn't even twitch. They mock you, O king."

Samlis, a chief magician, agreed. "The whole assembly has seen them. Unless you take immediate action, a rebellion could break out."

Nebuchadnezzar snarled. "Bring them to me!"

Several advisors grabbed the three Jews and forced them forward.

"Now," hissed Nardi, "we'll see whose god you worship!"

Nebuchadnezzar stared at Shadrach. "Again I say, at the moment you hear the sound of the music, fall down and worship my image. If you don't, I'll cast you into the pit of fire immediately! Do you understand?"

Shadrach glanced at his two friends. His face trembled. But he spoke without hesitation. "King Nebuchadnezzar, we offer no defense for our actions. We won't worship the idol. If our God desires, He is able to deliver us out of the furnace of fire. But even if He doesn't, we won't serve your gods or worship the golden image you've set up."

Nebuchadnezzar's forehead turned crimson and he lost his breath. "Who do you think you are, defying me like this?" He turned to an official and said, "Make the furnace seven times hotter than usual!"

Quickly, soldiers and workmen were gathered. They cast more charcoal and oil into a large opening at the bottom of the furnace. The flames blasted out of the hole on top. Shadrach watched calmly, although the heat felt like a wall before him.

Nebuchadnezzar glanced back and forth from the fire to the young men. Their calm only enraged him more. "Throw them in!" he shouted above the roar of the flames.

Three soldiers tied them up from head to foot. Then six more joined in to help carry them to the furnace. Shadrach smiled at his friends. "Today we meet our God."

Abednego replied, "More than that. Today we see His glory!"

The soldiers carried the men up the ramp. The huge hole spewed sparks and flames. But suddenly, Shadrach felt a strangely cool sensation. He looked at his friends, then at the soldiers. The soldiers grunted and heaved, their bodies sweating. But Abednego and Meshach were smiling.

Moments later, Shadrach landed with a thud in the center of the flames. But there was no sensation of pain or even warmth. He looked at Abednego and Meshach. "How can this be?" he shouted above the roar of the fire.

But he noticed his two friends looking past him. They fell on their faces. Shadrach turned. He knew instantly whom he was looking at. He fell on his face and worshiped.

The Angel of the Lord touched the three men and raised them to their feet. Shadrach and his friends spilled over with questions. Smiling, the Angel answered them slowly, directly. As He spoke, Shadrach sensed an inner light, a joy. As he listened, he worshiped.

And all because we obeyed, he thought.

Have you ever faced a choice between obeying God and obeying the world?

You might think that, in a land of freedom, we wouldn't have to face choices like that. After all, when was the last time someone demanded that you worship an idol? It just doesn't happen today, right? Wrong. It may surprise you to learn that the choice between obeying God or obeying man happens nearly every day.

• You're at a party. Someone waves around a vial of coke and offers everyone a snort. Everyone else lines up, but you stand back in a corner. Suddenly, all faces turn to look at you. Will you go their way or God's way?

• In the locker room, one of the guys begins bragging about a sexual experience he had with a girl. Someone asks you, "Have you done it yet?" Instantly you're tempted to lie and make up some juicy story. How *would* you reply?

● While driving to a concert, you realize you're going to be late. Three friends in the car try to get you to hurry and go over the speed limit. You refuse. They call you a jerk. How do you answer them?

● At the lunch table, people talk about a person behind her back. So far you've said nothing. Then someone turns to you and says, "She's such a _ _ _ _ _, isn't she?" What would you say?

These may seem like minor situations, but for many, they are big tests. "Will you go My way," the Lord is asking, "or theirs?"

What do you do in these types of circumstances? Do you go along with the crowd? Do you slide down in your seat and hope no one notices? Do you go ahead and do what you know is wrong, telling yourself, "God will forgive me; He understands"? Do you become angry with God, or the Bible, or other Christians, saying, "Why do I have to have these problems?" Or do you do right, accept the consequences, and rejoice in the opportunity to glorify God?

SOME PRINCIPLES

The story of Shadrach, Meshach, and Abednego offers us some insights that will help us stand up to the awesome test of obeying God rather than men.

A first insight is this: realize that you will face these choices—frequently—because God plans it that way! As it says in Jeremiah 17:10, "I the Lord search the heart and examine the mind, to reward a man according to his conduct, according to what his deeds deserve." God puts us in the furnace of tough choices to find out where we stand with Him.

We need to remember that nothing happens just to happen. Everything is planned. God "works out everything in conformity with the purpose of His will" (Ephesians 1:11).

What is God's purpose? That we might be transformed. And how will He transform us? By putting us in hot tubs, feeding us filet mignon, and always making us the hit of the party? Not likely. The way you transform someone is to put them through tests and run them through exercises. The football coach molds his players through a program of rigorous discipline. The tougher the conflict, the greater the development. Why should it be any different with God?

Right now, the reason you face hard choices is that God is developing your spiritual muscles. So don't complain about the tough spot you're in; rather, celebrate. He's making you into something splendid. Like Paul said, "In all these things we are more than conquerors through Him who loved us" (Romans 8:37). In what things? In tribulation, distress, persecution, famine, nakedness, peril, and sword—that's where you achieve an overwhelming victory, not in a hot tub!

A second insight we get from this story is that God isn't going to make you face the inferno until you've learned how to blow out a candle. That is, before you ever face a big test, God will put you through many little ones.

Daniel 3 is preceded by Daniel 1 and 2 (obviously). What happened in those chapters prepared Shadrach and his friends for the big test. In Daniel 1, we read how the young Jews decided not to eat meat sacrificed to idols. They asked the cook to feed them vegetables and water instead. It wasn't a monumental moment, but it was an important test. Before they could get on to the fiery furnace, they first had to avoid the fabulous food.

It's remarkable to me as a Christian just how well God has planned out our lives. He loves us so much that He has engineered every detail of our lives to work for good. When we get to heaven, we'll see the whole plan of God laid out and rejoice that He has indeed "done all things well."

We don't always respond favorably to those trials in which we're forced to choose between God and men, but we can learn from all of them. I've personally seen myself grow, become bolder, and develop confidence. I can see His transforming handiwork. That's not only a marvel, but a joy.

A third insight from this story is that when you face a difficult test, you should pray, obey, and expect that God will do what's best. We don't know all that Shadrach and his friends thought before they were cast into the fiery furnace, but I suspect that they spent time in prayer and meditation, asking God for wisdom. Like James says, when you're in a trial, don't ask why the trial is happening, but seek wisdom to learn how to deal with it (James 1:5-6).

Shadrach, Meshach, and Abednego made a very intriguing statement to Nebuchadnezzar. When the king ordered them the second time to worship, they replied that God was able to save them out of the king's hand. Bold words—but anyone could say that. What they follow it up with is an amazing statement: "But even if He does not, we want you to know, O king, that we will not serve your gods or worship the image of gold you have set up" (Daniel 3:18).

Look at those words. If you *know* God is going to save you, then sure, you'd do anything—walk across Niagara Falls on a tightrope, stand at ground zero during a nuclear test, jump off the Sears Tower in Chicago. But the problem is that we *don't know* if God will save us! That's the tough part. What if He doesn't? What if He'd let Shadrach, Meshach, and Abednego burn up? This statement was an incredible example of obedience and submission to God's will. It didn't matter whether God saved them or not. What mattered, from the standpoint of eternity, was their obedience to His will.

This is a difficult concept for us to understand. We thought all our friends would marvel at our courage when we refused to drink. But instead they avoid us and make fun of us. We figured that by saving ourselves until marriage, everything in our sex lives would be fantastic. But then we find that even decent girls think we're nerds because of it. We thought that by going to church and joining the youth group, we'd find true acceptance. But then we discover that the kids in the youth group can be just as bad as non-Christians. What do you do?

Like Shadrach, Meshach, and Abednego, you say: "I know my God can save me in a way I'd like; but even if He doesn't, I'll still obey Him because He's worthy and He'll ultimately reward me." Do you have that mentality? I hope so, because it's the only thing that will see you through the big decisions.

A fourth insight here is that the three men did not offer the king an explanation or defense for their action. This is a good principle for us to learn: stop trying to explain to unbelievers why you're obeying Christ; they won't (or can't) understand.

So often as Christians we try to explain to others why we do what we do. And what's usually their response? *"That's stupid." "Why do you feel that way?" "Oh, I'm sure God would understand if you didn't do that." "What a jerk."* People have fallen natures. Apart from the Spirit's work and leading, they simply can't understand God's ways.

Years before I became a Christian, a friend who worked in a sporting goods store had strung a tennis racket for me with merchandise from the store—at no charge. In other words, the string was stolen.

When I was converted, the Spirit brought this sin to

my mind. I was convicted, so I wrote a letter to the store with a check, and apologized (without revealing my friend's name—he had gone to another job). I thought that was the end of it. However, an employee recognized my name and called up a mutual friend, asking what was going on. Shortly afterward my friend called me and chewed me out about my action. "What are you trying to do—get everyone in trouble now with this Christian bit of yours? Forget this stuff. You can't go back and correct everything you did wrong."

At the time I responded with anger and tried to defend my action. But now I recognize the uselessness of it. My friend didn't understand; neither did the store; neither did many others. They offered plenty of reasons for me to simply overlook my long-forgotten crime. But I knew I had to obey the Lord in the matter.

So it was with Shadrach, Meshach, and Abednego. They just said to the king, "O Nebuchadnezzar, we do not need to defend ourselves before you in this matter" (Daniel 3:16). They were saying, "Yes, we're guilty of not bowing to the image. We can't try to defend it. We simply admit it."

Give up trying to offer an explanation for obedience to Christ. That doesn't mean you shouldn't ever defend the faith or what the Bible says. There is an appropriate time for a defense of one's actions. But in general, there's no point in constantly trying to explain to non-Christians why you do what you do. Don't give them fancy explanations; give them Christ. Only then will the explanations make sense.

A fifth insight from the story is that we should expect God to work things for His glory. In the end, God did save Shadrach, Meshach, and Abednego—in a way no one could have anticipated. He allowed them to walk safely with Him in the midst of the fiery furnace.

When they came out, their hair wasn't even singed! After that, the king ordered that everyone worship the true God and that if anyone spoke against Jehovah, that person would be torn limb from limb!

Isn't that incredible? The three young men not only passed a great test, but God was glorified in a way that led to conversions, change, promotion, and honor.

That doesn't mean God will be always glorified in a way that will be pleasant for us. Sometimes God is glorified through a horrible death. I think of John Hus, who was burned at the stake. Almost the same thing happened to him as to the three Jews in Daniel 3—except John Hus died. But one note on his death: it's written that he died singing! God was glorified, though in a different way.

Or take the stories in Kefa Sempangi's book, *A Distant Grief*, about the ordeal of Christians in Idi Amin's Uganda. Sempangi writes of a famous Ugandan businessman and leader who became a Christian. One day Amin himself confronted him about his faith. After hours of torture, this great Christian was murdered by being smashed with hammers. What a horrid death! Was Amin converted? No. Were others? Possibly. Yet, was God glorified? Absolutely. We may not see all the ways. But in at least one, we see that people were forced to face the fact that a man was willing to die rather than deny his God. That speaks highly of the man, and even more highly of his God.

God is in the business of making His name and person known. He will do it through the Shadrachs, Meshachs, and Abednegos of this world. He will also do it through you—if you let Him.

2

SOLOMON

IF GOD OFFERED YOU ANYTHING

Abigail awakened to the chirps of birds outside her door. She yawned and smiled, and snuggled in the warmth under the blankets. She glanced at her new baby, Joshua, and giggled. "I never thought it would be such a marvel," she said.

The baby made no movement or sound. Abigail smoothed his curly black hair and pulled him up to her bosom. The baby felt stiff.

She pulled him from under the covers. "Joshua! JOSHUA!" She shook him in the air. No response. The baby was dead.

Abigail screamed. "Rachel! RACHEL!"

Her friend strolled casually into the room. "Yes?"

"It's Joshua. He's—he's dead! Look." She wiped her eyes and held out the dark, stiff form in her lap. "How could this happen? He was just . . . " She began crying.

Rachel shrugged. "Oh, well. Maybe you'll have another." The sound of her baby's cries rose in the other room. She turned and walked out.

Abigail stared at her, astonished. Then she looked

at Joshua's face. He didn't look much like—

Suddenly, Abigail jumped up. "This isn't Joshua!"

She ran into the other room and stared at Rachel as she held her baby, Eliah. Rachel's lips flickered a smile as she sang to the baby.

Abigail marched over to her. "Let me see Eliah."

Rachel pulled him close, covering his head. "Go back to your dead Joshua. I'll take care of my baby."

"Let me see him," Abigail said fiercely.

Rachel held him out reluctantly.

Abigail tried to pull him out of Rachel's arms. "This is Joshua, my baby. Eliah died in the night and you switched them. How dare you!"

Rachel fought back, pulling Joshua away. "This is my baby and I'm keeping him," she said evenly. "It's my word against yours."

Abigail stormed out the door. "I'll take it to the elders!" she cried. "They'll know what to do."

Hours later, the elders near the gate of the city stood rubbing their chins, puzzled. They were not sure which woman was telling the truth. Rachel seemed more in control of her emotions, more cool about it all. Abigail was hysterical. But which one was lying?

Finally, Eliakim, one of the elders, said, "Perhaps we should take this to the elders in Jerusalem. All of the harder cases go to them. I understand they're very fair." The others agreed.

Unfortunately, though, the Jerusalem elders were no better. They too were baffled by the women's accounts. The chief elder finally sighed. "Perhaps King Solomon is our only hope."

Suddenly, everyone stopped talking and looked at the chief elder.

"King Solomon?" said Eliakim with wide eyes.

The chief elder nodded. "This is a very difficult

case. There are no witnesses, no proof, nothing."

The women were brought into the throne room. King Solomon was only twenty-one years old, but already had proved that he was wise and fair.

The king listened to both stories. He glanced from woman to woman, rubbing his chin and watching their eyes.

Abigail concluded, "I don't know how it happened, my king. I only know I went to sleep with Joshua, and now this—"she paused and looked at Rachel angrily—"this so-called friend of mine has cheated me."

The king nodded. He turned to the cupbearer on his right. "Bring in a swordsman."

Abigail breathed deeply. Her heart pounded in her chest. Why would he want a swordsman? "Oh, please let the truth be known," she prayed in her heart.

The swordsman came in.

"Take the baby from the woman," the king said to a second soldier. He took it gently from her hand.

"Hold the baby up," Solomon said. "This is my decree. The swordsman will divide the baby in two and each woman will get a half."

One of the elders stifled a laugh, but Solomon held up his hand. "I do not make jokes," he said.

Everyone was quiet.

"Each woman, as I said, will have half."

Abigail gasped when she realized the king was serious. "But the baby will die!"

"And each of you will have a half," said Solomon again, smiling.

Abigail shook her head. "But that will kill him," she said. Tears filled her eyes. She swallowed and stared at the king. "Please, my lord, please don't kill the baby. Let the other woman have him. I'd rather that he live . . . " She put her face in her hands and wept. She looked up again. The swordsman had poised the sword above the child's head.

Abigail ran forward and fell to her knees before the king. "Please, my king, let Rachel have the child. Just let him live."

Rachel's lips curled. "The king's judgment is best," she said with hard, searing words. "The baby shall be neither mine nor yours. Divide him."

Solomon held up his hand. "Put down your sword." He glanced from Rachel to Abigail who was still at his feet, her eyes red from weeping.

"Give the child to Abigail. She is his mother." He took her hand and pulled her to her feet. The swordsman put the baby in her arms.

The king touched Abigail on the shoulder. "He is a handsome baby. You will be a good mother. Go in peace."

Her eyes again filled with tears and she bowed. "Thank you so much," she said.

Eliakim turned and whispered to the other elders, "If he settles more cases as easily as this, his kingdom will be the greatest on earth."

SOLOMON'S WISDOM

You'll find the story of how Solomon received his great wisdom in 1 Kings 3:2-15. There had been a long and painful struggle between him and his brother, Adonijah, to determine who would succeed David as the next king. Solomon won.

So here he was, only twenty years old, and the head of an important kingdom in the Near East. Solomon understood, though, that his youth and inexperience could topple his kingdom. He cried out for God's help, approval, and guidance. Shortly after that, God appeared to Solomon in a dream. He said, "Ask for whatever you want Me to give you" (1 Kings 3:5).

Imagine having such an offer from God! "Ask for

whatever you want!" Whatever. No requests denied. It seems incredible, doesn't it? What would you ask for? Wealth? Power? Beauty? Long life? Fame? World peace?

You name it, Solomon could have had it. So what did he choose? It's revealed in verse 9: "So give Your servant a discerning heart to govern Your people and to distinguish between right and wrong. For who is able to govern this great people of Yours?"

BREAKING IT DOWN

Let's take that a little more slowly. Basically, Solomon asked for one thing with three elements:

What? A discerning heart.

What for? To govern God's people.

With what ultimate result? To distinguish between right and wrong.

A "discerning" heart actually means a "hearing" heart. A hearing heart is one that sees beneath the surface, one that looks with insight into people, situations, and God. Solomon wanted to be able to understand with depth. He wanted to know what lay beneath the surface. He longed to see "into" things and understand motives, thoughts, plans, ideas—the things that drove and guided men to do what they did.

Why did he want it? So that he could govern the people of Israel. Being a leader requires much wisdom, character, and ability. Solomon wanted this kind of understanding so that he would govern fairly and kindly. He wanted his subjects' love. But more than that, he wanted their respect.

Then what was his ultimate goal? To be able to look at a situation, no matter how confusing, and sift through both the evil and good elements. As in the case of the two women, he wanted to see where the good ended and the evil began.

GOOD FOR SOLOMON, BUT WHAT ABOUT ME?

Well, that's all very nice for Solomon. God gave him an offer he couldn't refuse. Somehow he had the smarts to ask for wisdom. Great. But what about us? None of us have had God pop into our dreams, offering us anything. Right?

Actually, God *does* offer us an opportunity like He offered Solomon, but it's not an open-ended proposition. God offers to give us the same kind of wisdom as Solomon, if we'll just ask.

● "If any of you lacks wisdom, he should ask God, who gives generously to all without finding fault and it will be given to him" (James 1:5). When God gives you wisdom, He gives you the genuine thing, the same type that He has, and He gives it abundantly and gladly.

● "Ask and it will be given to you; seek and you will find; knock and the door will be opened to you" (Matthew 7:7). This verse is actually a commentary on how God answers prayer. Sometimes all you have to do is ask, and He serves up the answer.

But occasionally you have to "put legs" on your prayers. You have to go out and try to *find* what you've been praying for. For instance, if you pray that God will help you find a job, you have to go out and look for one.

But sometimes there's even more required: knocking. You have to bang on some doors to get what you want. Not every door opens. But when God's ready to answer, the right one will open.

What does this have to do with wisdom? Wisdom works the same way. Sometimes God just infuses our minds with the right answers and knowledge. We simply *know* what to do in a certain situation.

But occasionally, if we want wisdom about something, we have to seek, study, work, observe, and make some effort. If you're struggling with the issue of how to love the person you're dating without compromising God's will about sex, you may need to open your Bible and pore over its pages for a while. The answer might not simply *occur* to you.

Finally, much wisdom requires knocking. You have to ask around, counsel, study, and really work it through. Wisdom about evangelism is like that. You may want to witness to your friends, but you don't know how. What do you do? You read books, study, and work at it. Then you start knocking on doors. Eventually, some will open. In the process, you store up a lot of wisdom.

● "If you remain in Me and My words remain in you, ask whatever you wish, and it will be given you" (John 15:7). This statement looks strangely like what God said to Solomon when He offered him anything he desired. Is Jesus saying He'll give us anything we want? Yes, but there is one condition.

"If we 'remain' in Him and His words 'remain' in us." What does that mean?

"Remain" means to abide, or stay in the presence of. That's fairly simple. Jesus is saying, "If you walk with Me and stay with Me day by day, and if My Word stays in you—that is, if it influences and guides and directs all that you do—then ask whatever you wish."

"But what if I asked to be rich—would He do it?"

Could you ask for wealth if you knew all that His Word says about it? Could you ask for it if day by day you've been walking with and learning of Him? Probably not, because the closer you get to Jesus, the more you think and act like Him. If you find yourself wanting the things of this world, that may be an indication that you're not walking with Him.

That's the key. God gives wisdom only when we abide in His Word and walk with Christ. He'll bless our lives only when we obey Him.

I find that one of my own most frequent prayers is for wisdom—wisdom to know how to deal with problems and situations; wisdom to live properly and happily; wisdom to lead my family and nurture my wife and children. I'm always asking for wisdom in one form or another.

And God answers. Not always the way I expect, and not always on my schedule—but the wisdom comes. Eventually I see what should be done.

HOW DOES HIS WISDOM COME?

How then will you gain the wisdom God wants to give? Let me offer you some scriptural ways to gain wisdom.

1. Through meditation on God's Word

Psalm 119:97-100 are four verses that are very special to me: "Oh, how I love your law! I meditate on it all day long. Your commands make me wiser than my enemies, for they are ever with me. I have more insight than all my teachers, for I meditate on your statutes. I have more understanding than the elders, for I obey your precepts."

First, meditation results in wisdom. That's skill for life, the ability to see the best course in the midst of a problem.

Second, meditation results in insight—*more than all my teachers*. What do teachers do? They teach us about things, how they work, what makes them tick. Insight is the ability to see inside, to know what makes people and things operate, what motivates them. Anyone who has that kind of insight, that kind of "people smarts," will go a long way in this world.

Finally, meditation results in understanding—*more*

than the elders. What can elders do? Since they've learned about life, they can see it all in perspective. They can put it all together and make sense of it. That's understanding—to see beyond the moment, the week, even the lifetime; to see what God's doing and to understand why.

Do you want those things? Then meditate on His Word. Memorize verses of Scripture, then think about them. Pick them apart. Define the terms. Figure out what they're saying. Then apply them to your life. Through this process, you will gain wisdom.

2. Through study

Paul told Timothy, "Do your best to present yourself to God as one approved, a workman who does not need to be ashamed and who correctly handles the word of truth" (2 Timothy 2:15).

The key to understanding this verse is to study the verse that comes before it and the verse that comes after it. Second Timothy 2:14 speaks of not "quarreling about words; it is of no value and only ruins those who listen." Paul meant, "Get rid of the word battles, where everyone just gives his opinion about what something means. Rather, find out clearly what it means, and be accurate. Then people will learn."

That's the first thing: study. Find out the facts. Learn the truth. Don't just become a dabbler in opinions.

Second Timothy 2:16 says, "Avoid godless chatter, because those who indulge in it will become more and more ungodly."

"Godless chatter." Isn't that what we hear all day— gossip, arguments, discussions about foolish things? Paul says, "Spend your time in study so that you're accurate, so that you know what you're talking about."

That's a key to wisdom. If you want it, you'll have to study, to get down into the text, to mine out the silver and gold.

3. Through observation

Another interesting passage is Proverbs 24:30-34. In those verses, Solomon tells of how he passed by a field owned by a lazy man. The vine was overgrown with thistles, and there were weeds all over the place. The stone wall was a shambles. Solomon thought about it. "What can I learn from this?" he asked himself. Then he came to a conclusion: "A little sleep, a little slumber, a little folding of the hands to rest—and poverty will come on you like a bandit, and scarcity like an armed man." In other words, "Get lazy slowly—get poor suddenly!"

Are you an observer of life? Do you spend time watching people, how they talk, how they respond, how they act? Do you take those observations and set them down as principles about life?

That's another key to wisdom—observation. Watch what's happening around you. Don't just let it happen. Otherwise, you'll be an example of the saying: "Some people make it happen; some people let it happen; and some people don't know what's happening!"

4. Through listening to your elders

Oh, what a tough one! Listening to your mom and dad, grandma and grandpa, aunt and uncle—it's critical. Solomon advised, "Listen, my sons, to a father's instruction; pay attention and gain understanding" (Proverbs 4:1). The Book of Proverbs is full of those kind of exhortations. Solomon had to appeal to his sons to listen to him.

Do you ever think that Dad and Mom haven't got a sensible cell in their brains? Then you're probably afflicted with the "I-know-more-than-you" syndrome. It afflicts most of us from ages thirteen to nineteen. We begin to think we know it all. "No one's going to tell me what to do. And if they do, watch out!"

Yet parents can be a rich source of wisdom and understanding about life. When I was nineteen, I had a 1965 Ford Mustang—four on the floor, cream finish, 289 cubes, four barrel—a real mean machine. One snowy winter day, I turned a corner and couldn't stop soon enough to avoid the car ahead of me. I wrecked my Mustang. The front end of my beloved car looked like a boxer who had just fought Mike Tyson and had taken it on the chin.

The car could still be driven, though, and I went to a gas station to call my father. When he answered, I told him what had happened. His first words were, "Is everyone all right?"

I kept telling him about the car. "The whole front end is smashed (sniff, sniff) and it looks awful and I can barely drive it and—"

Dad broke in. "Is everyone OK?"

"I mean the headlight's out and the bumper's all twisted up and—"

Dad shouted this time. "IS EVERYBODY ALL RIGHT?"

I stopped in midsentence. Then I said, "Yes, everyone's fine. But my car, the front is—"

Dad said, "Mark, cars can be fixed. People can't. If everyone's OK, that's all that matters."

At the time I didn't think Dad understood. But about five years later, I realized what he'd said. It's taken me a while to learn that people are more important than things. But that was one piece of wisdom my father gave me.

5. Through seeking it constantly

You want wisdom? Then seek it constantly. Solomon said it this way: "My son, if you accept my words and store up my commands within you, turning your ear to wisdom and applying your heart to understanding, and if you call out for insight and cry aloud for understanding, and if you look for it as for silver and search for it as for hidden treasure, then you will understand the fear of the Lord and find the knowledge of God" (Proverbs 2:1-5).

Sometimes God gives wisdom only to those who press after it like a thirsty deer searching for water. You have to go for it, want it more than anything else. Then you shall have it.

There's an old story about a proud young man who came to Socrates asking for knowledge. He walked up to the muscular, bald-headed philosopher and said, "O great Socrates, I come to you for knowledge."

Socrates was one of the wisest men of his time and he recognized a pompous numbskull when he saw one. He motioned for the young man to follow him. They walked to the sea. Socrates led the young man out into the chest-deep water. Then he asked, "What do you want?"

"Knowledge, O wise Socrates," said the young man with a smile.

Socrates put his strong hands on the lad's shoulders and thrust him under the water. The lad struggled.

Thirty seconds later, Socrates let him up.

"What do you want?" he asked again.

The boy sputtered, "Wisdom, O great and wise Socrates."

Socrates pushed him under again. Thirty seconds. Thirty-five. Forty.

He let him up. The boy was coughing. "What do you want, young man?"

Between heavy, heaving breaths the boy said, "Knowledge, O wise and wonderful—"

Socrates jammed him under again. Forty seconds. He let him up again.

"What do you want?"

"Air!" sputtered the youth. "I need air."

Socrates waited. When they'd both calmed down, he said, "When you want knowledge as you have just wanted air, then you will have knowledge."

When it comes to wisdom, couldn't we all use a little dunking now and then?

3

RUTH

A PICTURE OF COMMITMENT

The doctor gently touched the open eyes of Mahlon and pushed the eyelids downward. "I'm sorry, Ruth. He's dead."

Ruth stood, biting her lip. Tears streamed from her eyes.

Behind her, Naomi, her mother-in-law, wailed loudly. "Jehovah took my husband, then Kilion, and now Mahlon. I have lost everything."

Ruth fell into Naomi's arms, saying nothing. The two women walked out of the small room and into the sunshine.

Ruth tried to think. *What am I to do now? Naomi is a Hebrew. The Moabites will never accept her.*

She knew she could just as well leave Naomi on her own. But something within her said, *No, I must be loyal.*

Yet, as she looked across the parched land, she felt confused and frightened. Even *she* might not be accepted by the Moabites, her people, since she had married a Hebrew.

No, she said to herself, *it will be all right. We will*

find a way. All three of us. She glanced up at Orpah, her sister-in-law, who stood off to the side. She wondered what Orpah must be thinking, having lost her own husband only two weeks before. Why hadn't they *all* died? Why had Jehovah let the women live, if this was the way they had to live?

Ruth forced those thoughts from her mind. "Come," she said to Naomi and Orpah, "we need something to eat. The days ahead will not be easy."

A week later, Naomi called her two daughters-in-law into the main room of the house. "I am going back to Judah. There are reports that the famine has ended."

Ruth and Orpah nodded. "We will go with you," they said.

Naomi gazed at them with pursed lips, but said nothing.

They packed their belongings, then started down the main road to Judah. After several miles they came upon a hill. When they reached the top, they could see Judah. Noami put her bags down.

"It's no good," she said to Ruth and Orpah. "There is no reason for you to come. My people will not easily accept Moabite women. Go, each of you back to your mother's house. I pray the Lord will deal kindly with you the way you've dealt with me. May the Lord grant that you find rest, each in the house of a husband."

Suddenly, Ruth said, "No, we'll both go to Judah and be with your people."

Orpah nodded her head.

Naomi said, "No, please. Do you think I can provide husbands for you? What good am I to you? Would you wait for me to have sons so you could marry them?"

Ruth knew Naomi was beyond the age of childbearing. Ruth began to speak, but Naomi stopped her.

"This is harder for me than you, but I know it's best. God's hand has gone against me. Do you think it will be any different in Judah?"

The three women wept together. Afterward, Orpah picked up her bundles and left.

Naomi gazed at Ruth. "Go on. Go back to your mother's house. There's more hope—"

Suddenly Ruth fell into Naomi's arms. "I will not go. Please stop telling me to go. I want to be with you. Wherever you go, I'll go."

Naomi shook her head. "You don't know what you're saying. I'm miserable. Why should two of us be miserable?"

Ruth bit her lip. "I'm going with you. Wherever you go, I'll go. Wherever you live, I'll live. Your people will be my people, and your God, my God. Wherever you die, I will die and I'll be buried beside you. If I don't do this, may the Lord deal with me, if anything but death parts us."

Naomi gazed at her face a long time. She looked up and shielded her eyes from the sun. "You may never marry again."

"So be it," said Ruth.

"We will have to work hard to get even a few grains of wheat."

Ruth nodded. "So be it."

Naomi pursed her lips. "You're determined to do this?"

Ruth nodded. She felt her heart thundering inside her breast.

"All right. Come."

Together they wept again, then picked up their bags and walked toward Judah.

The story of Ruth won't go down as a dramatic moment in history. First of all, it's about a daughter-in-law's love for her mother-in-law. On a scale of one to ten for the most interesting subjects to discuss in church, that ranks about a minus fourteen.

Secondly, the story lacks the sparkle of a powerful plot. "Woman loses husband and two sons. She decides to leave land. Daughter-in-law says she'll go with her." What's that? Not even soap operas would use that kind of melodrama.

Thirdly, Ruth is far too submissive. She does everything her mother-in-law tells her to do. Who wants to hear about a woman who obeys her mother-in-law?

Of course, you're probably wondering what this has to do with you as a high school student. You'd probably rather study something with a bit more flair, like David knocking off Goliath (although that one is a little old too).

But strangely enough, Ruth provides for us some keen insight into an important issue: what does it mean to follow Jesus Christ?

PLENTY OF CONTROVERSY

There's plenty of controversy today among Christians about salvation, lordship, and obedience to Christ. Many people wonder just what is necessary for one to be saved. Is it simply walking down an aisle, praying a prayer, and signing on the dotted line? Can someone claim to be a Christian simply because he or she prayed a certain prayer, and then live like the devil after that?

That's what some people say. They argue that salvation is totally of grace. There are no strings attached. Just receive the present, and go on your merry way. Of course, it would be nice if you obeyed the Lord, or tried to be a disciple, or repented of your sins. But none of those things are necessary to get into the kingdom.

Is that true? If it isn't, there may be millions out there who have been deceived into thinking they're saved when in reality they're just as lost as they ever were.

With that in mind, let's look at the story of Ruth as a picture of salvation.

TRAITS OF TRUE COMMITMENT

Admittedly, Naomi had had a hard time of it. First, famine struck the land of Judah, so her husband decided to move to Moab, an enemy country. Pulling up roots and leaving everything was hard enough. But then after settling in the new land, her husband, Elimelech, died. Next, her two sons, Mahlon and Kilion, married Moabite women. This would make Naomi's own grandchildren half-breeds, and subject to all the rejection that such people face.

But Naomi never even had a chance to have grandchildren. Her two sons died too. Understandably, she became bitter, feeling that God was against her. She had lost nearly everything.

When she decided to return to Judah because the famine had ended, she knew the right thing to do: leave her sons' wives behind. She would free them from whatever obligation they had to her, and then all three of them could start over. Her intent was noble and understandable.

Eventually, Orpah did return to her people. But for some reason, Ruth decided to stay with Naomi and go with her to Judah. What that reason was is never revealed. Perhaps it came down to the fact that she loved Naomi.

But love alone was not enough to make Ruth leave her people, her homeland, her own family, and everything she knew to go to a distant and hostile place.

So what was it that compelled Ruth to cling to her

mother-in-law? I believe it was the Lord Jesus Christ Himself. God had placed a call on Ruth's life. (She eventually married Boaz and became one of the physical ancestors of Jesus.)

Let me give you five elements that characterize a true commitment to Christ, as is pictured in the relationship of Ruth and Naomi.

1. Unwavering determination

Notice what Ruth said to Naomi in her majestic statement of commitment to her. "Don't urge me to leave you or to turn back from you" (Ruth 1:16). It's obvious this woman is determined. She's saying, "Please don't try to talk me out of it, because I've already made up my mind."

I often see this lacking in the so-called commitments to Christ that happen in our churches. There's no determination, no "I've-got-to-do-it" spirit. How does that square with such Scripture as, "Anyone who does not take his cross and follow Me is not worthy of Me"? (Matthew 10:38) Taking up a cross was something the Romans forced criminals who were about to be executed to do. When you saw a person going down the road, carrying a cross, it meant only one thing: he was going to die.

In the same way, Jesus meant that a person who wanted to follow Him had to be finished with everything in this life. The follower had to be as good as dead to the world.

Jesus told a parable about such determination. A pearl merchant longed for the one pearl that was greater than all others. One day he found it. It was terrifically expensive. But he sold all that he had and bought it (Matthew 13:45-46).

That's determination. That's how much Scripture says we should want salvation. We should be willing to sell everything—to give our very lives to Christ—in order that we might have it. Like Jesus said, "If anyone comes to Me and does not hate his father and mother, his wife and children, his brothers and sisters—yes, and his own life—he cannot be My disciple" (Luke 14:26).

That was the kind of determination Ruth had toward her mother-in-law, Naomi. "Don't try to stop me or deter me. I've made up my mind. I'm coming with you." Do you have that kind of determination to follow Christ?

2. A new direction, a new submission

The next statement Ruth makes is even more dramatic in the context of the book. She says to Naomi, "Where you go, I will go, and where you stay, I will stay." She would no longer do as she pleased with her life. Her life from that point on would be a submissive following in Naomi's footsteps.

I believe this is similar to the repentance and submission to Christ that comes with true salvation. What do we find in the preaching of Christ and others in the Bible? "Repent, for the kingdom of heaven is near." John the Baptist baptized people for repentance as they confessed their sins (Matthew 3:6). Jesus told the Pharisees when they saw Him dining with tax collectors and sinners, "I have not come to call the righteous, but sinners to repentance" (Luke 5:32). When Peter preached to the crowd on the day of Pentecost and told them about Jesus' death and resurrection, the people asked what they should do. He answered, "Repent, and be baptized, every one of you, in the name of Jesus Christ so that your sins may be forgiven" (Acts 2:38). When Paul spoke before King Agrippa, explaining the purpose of his preaching, he summarized his message to lost men with these words,

"They should repent and turn to God and prove their repentance by their deeds" (Acts 26:20).

Clearly, repentance involves a change of heart, mind, and lifestyle. You begin to go in a whole new direction. You look at your old life and sin and say, "I don't want to follow that course anymore. I'm taking a new direction—with Jesus."

Moreover, there's a new submission to Jesus Christ as well. Jesus told His listeners to "take My yoke upon you and learn from Me" (Matthew 11:29). Taking a yoke for a cow or bull was an act of submission to the farmer. Our yoke means coming under Christ's authority.

Paul told the Corinthians, "If anyone is in Christ, he is a new creation" (2 Corinthians 5:17). That involves a change of life, a submission and obedience to Christ.

John said, "The man who says, 'I know Him,' but does not do what He commands is a liar" (1 John 2:4). What is doing what He commands, except obedience and submission?

It's simply unavoidable. True Christianity involves the kind of turning and change of direction that Ruth exemplified. She was leaving the old life and the old ways, and embarking on a new life, in faith. Many so-called Christians overlook this teaching. They say that salvation in Christ has nothing to do with repentance and obedience, which supposedly come *after* you're saved.

What I'm saying here is that these things are all part of the process of salvation. *God* does it in the believer. It's not something we work up, or decide to do. It's something He produces in us in the process of saving us. "For it is God who works in you to will and to act according to His good pleasure" (Philippians 2:13).

Consider the nature of salvation. Is it simply the promise that if you believe in Christ you'll go to heaven when you die? If that is so, then why did Jesus say, "I have come that they may have life, and have it to the full"? (John 10:10)

Actually, salvation is much more than that. It's (1) forgiveness of past, present, and future sins; (2) eternal life—both quality and quantity of life; (3) being transferred from the kingdom of darkness to the kingdom of light; and (4) being transformed from a sinner to a saint. It involves a great many other things too, but that's the essence. That fourth thing—transformation—is an ongoing process that will be completed either at death or the Rapture, whichever comes first for the individual believer.

3. A new family

Ruth brought up a third element of commitment to Christ when she said to Naomi, "Your people will be my people."

This is one of the first things that strikes a new Christian—the sense of being part of something new, a new family, having new friends who believe similarly to you. It was one of the greatest joys for me as a new Christian to find kindred spirits everywhere in the church. Suddenly, I found whole groups of people who felt the same way as I about the most basic issues of life: "Who am I?"; "Where am I going?"; "What is life all about?"; "Is there a God?"; "Who is He?"; "Can I know Him?"

One of the most striking things I discovered as a new Christian was that with my new friends there was often a deeper and more open love than with those of my own family. I could discuss the deep concerns of my heart with them. They seemed to listen and care in ways I hadn't seen with non-Christian friends. They also had a much sharper concern for heart and eternal matters than any non-Christian.

Of course, Christians are sinners too, and can make shattering errors in their treatment of the brethren. They can be judgmental, nasty, unloving, hypocritical, and ungodly. Someone has said that the church is the only army that shoots its own wounded. That can be very true.

But in another sense, you will also never find fellowship and the depth of love in the world that you find in the church.

When I went through a terrible time of depression as a seminary student, I reached a point where I thought I might commit suicide. I asked my doctor to put me in a hospital. I was in for a month. While I was there, I met a number of people who suffered from agonizing mental disorders. One day I was talking with a young woman who was in for drug addiction. She commented to me, "It's very impressive all the visitors you get around here, Mark."

I asked what she meant. She said, "Since you've been in, there has been a constant stream of people to visit you. I'd like to know where they all come from."

I explained that they were from my church and the seminary I was attending. She said, "Well, it's really amazing. I never saw so many people who cared about someone in the hospital. You're very lucky."

At the time I was too depressed to feel any joy about her comment. But now I see the point. My friends wrote letters, gave me money to help pay medical bills, stayed up with me during the dark hours of depression between midnight and dawn, and came by my room just to cheer me up. Believe me, I wasn't a very cheery person to be around. But that didn't stop them. They didn't give up on me. I was glad to be a part of God's family.

Do you sense that you have a new family? That's part of true commitment to Christ.

4. A new Lord

Ruth goes on to say, "Your God [shall be] my God."

People today have little understanding of the gravity of Ruth's statement. What it actually meant was that her blood relatives would consider her dead for having left her gods. It was an amazing commitment that she was willing to leave it all to follow Naomi's God, Jehovah.

This is an important element of true salvation. Too often, new Christians bring certain elements of their old religion with them when they become Christians. For instance, Catholics continue such things as confession, saying the rosary, and doing penance for sin. Ex-Moslems might bring in their traditional practices. In such places as Haiti and other mission areas where there is a strong witchcraft influence, there is sometimes a mingling of Christianity and other practices.

This is lethal to a real walk with Jesus. Even the early church fell prey to this with such Jewish practices as circumcision, not eating with Gentiles, and keeping the Law. Many of Paul's letters were written to correct this improper mixing of traditions.

When we become Christians, we must leave the old gods behind—whether they be the abstract gods of selfishness and materialism, or whether they're the actual religions of Hinduism, Islam, Judaism, or others. God will not tolerate our mixing it up. " 'Therefore come out from them and be separate,' says the Lord. Touch no unclean thing, and I will receive you. I will be a Father to you, and you will be my sons and daughters, says the Lord Almighty' " (2 Corinthians 6:17-18).

I once had a friend in college whom I tried desperately to lead to Christ. One day he said to me, "Do you know what's holding me back from becoming a Christian?"

I was instantly interested.

He said, "I'm a virgin."

I was shocked—not that he was a virgin; on the contrary, I told him he should praise God he *was* one—but that such a thing could hold anyone from making a commitment to Christ.

He explained to me that until he'd lost his virginity he didn't think he could ever become a Christian, because he knew if he became one, he'd no longer be allowed to pursue that goal. His god, in a sense, was sex, and the loss of virginity. It was all he thought about. It obsessed him. He worshiped at the altar of sexual relations and followed after that desire.

My friend, sixteen years later, is no longer a virgin. He's also not a Christian.

What about you? Have you left your old gods behind?

5. A lifelong commitment

Ruth concludes her words to Naomi by saying, "Where you die I will die, and there I will be buried. May the Lord deal with me, be it ever so severely, if anything but death seperates you and me" (Ruth 1:17). She was saying, "This is a lifelong commitment, Naomi. There's no turning back."

Jesus said something similar: "No one who puts his hand to the plow and looks back is fit for service in the kingdom of God" (Luke 9:62). He said this in response to a disciple who said, "I will follow you, Lord, but first permit me to say good-bye to those at home." Why was Jesus so emphatic? Because I suspect that that young man wanted to go home and discuss what he was about to do with his family. You can almost hear the conversation.

"Well, what do you think, Dad—should I follow Jesus?"

Dad wrinkles up his face and asks some questions. "How much time will this take from your chores? Where will you live? What about when your mother and I get old?"

In a few minutes, the young man would probably have been talked out of his commitment.

That's precisely what Jesus was seeking to avoid. He was saying to the young man, "When you decide to plow a field, you can't put your hand on the plow and then turn back to look wishfully on all your other playthings. No, you set your face on the furrow and plow ahead."

Similarly, commitment to Christ is for life. There are no paroles, no three-year sentences. It's all or nothing.

Where then do you find yourself? Is your commitment to Christ an unwavering determination? A new direction and submission? A new family? A new God? A lifelong commitment?

Can it be anything less in light of what Jesus did for you?

4

JOSEPH

PASSING UP A CHANCE FOR REVENGE

So many hungry people, Joseph thought as he watched the crowd file by to purchase grain. *If not for the hand of God, even Egypt would have perished during this famine.*

For nearly a year now he had directed the sale of grain to the thousands who came to Egypt. It had been a long journey for Joseph: sold into slavery by his own brothers; unjustly accused of rape by his master's wife; thrown into prison; interpreting Pharaoh's remarkable dreams of seven years of plenty and seven years of famine.

How it had all happened was nothing less than astonishing. Now, more than ever, Joseph was convinced God could do anything.

As he gazed on the crowd, his eyes fixed on a small group of men approaching the throne. They were Semites, that was obvious. He looked deeply into their faces. *It can't be,* he thought.

Then one of them spoke to another in a foreign tongue. Joseph recognized the words. It was his own language, the one he grew up speaking.

Joseph fell back in his seat. These men were his ten brothers, the ten who had betrayed him! He had not seen them in twenty years.

He watched them move forward in line. Apparently, they hadn't recognized him. And why should they? Back then he was just a boy, seventeen years old. Now he was Prime Minister of Egypt.

His mind jumped back twenty years to the scene of their last meeting. He had been searching for his brothers that day, clothed in the beautiful coat his father had given him. He knew even then how his brothers hated him. They wouldn't speak to him on friendly terms.

When he finally found them, he sensed something was wrong. As he approached the group, Judah suddenly sprang forward, grabbing Joseph's arm, and wrenching it behind his back.

"So what should we do with you now, dreamer?" He motioned to Dan, who was holding a knife in his right hand. "Maybe you can dream how you'll escape from this."

Joseph tried to wriggle free, but Judah was too strong for him. When Dan stepped forward, Joseph realized his brothers planned to kill him. Just then, Reuben jumped forward.

"Stop!" he cried. "This isn't the way."

Judah retorted, "Now's our chance, Reuben. We can make up an excuse to tell Father."

Reuben shook his head and pulled Joseph away from Judah. "We don't have to kill him."

"Then what will we do?"

Reuben pointed to a nearby pit. "Throw him in there. Let's think about this before we do something we can't undo."

The other brothers reluctantly agreed.

Waiting in the pit, Joseph listened to them arguing.

Why can't there be peace between us? he thought. *This hatred is senseless.*

When his brothers came back later and pulled him out of the pit, Joseph saw another group of men, obviously from a caravan, standing about, eyeing him. Judah tore Joseph's cloak off and threw it to the ground. He turned to the group of men. "How much for him?"

They haggled about the price for a few minutes. When they finally agreed, Joseph was tied up and placed in the caravan, bound for Egypt.

As Joseph sat there on the royal seat in the grain room remembering those months and years, a choking sensation came over him. He began coughing. An aide rushed forward, but Joseph motioned him away. "I'm all right," he said in flawless Egyptian. He stared again at his ten brothers. They were next in line to dicker over the price of the grain. What should he do?

He could tell them who he was right away. *No,* he thought. *They aren't ready. They'd be afraid.*

He wanted to ask them so many questions. Were his father and younger brother still alive? What story had the ten made up to explain his disappearance? How had his father reacted?

There was a tightness in his throat. He closed his eyes and bit his lip. *How can I find out?* he asked himself. He groped in his mind for a possible plan. He couldn't let them know immediately. That would be too risky. They might refuse to reveal anything. They might flee. He wanted cooperation, not a repeat of their last encounter.

Judah stood before them. He was still the spokesman, still the brash leader. He began his plea and addressed the translator. Joseph understood his words, but pretended not to. Judah said, "We have come for grain. We can pay well."

Joseph waited for the translation. Immediately he retorted, "You're spies. You've come into the land to map out its undefended parts."

The translator interpreted. Judah's face fell. The ten men murmured among themselves.

Judah answered plaintively, "No, my lord, we've only come to buy food. We're all sons of one man. We're honest men. We haven't come to spy."

Joseph answered more firmly and harshly, asserting again they were spies.

Reuben stepped forward. "Sir, we are twelve brothers. Our father lives in Canaan. The youngest one is still with him. And one of us is no more."

So his father was still alive! Joseph felt himself jolt with happiness. But he let nothing show on his face. He waited for the translation, then stood up and folded his arms over his chest. "I don't believe you. But I'll give you a test. I won't let you leave unless your youngest brother comes here. One of you may go and get him. The rest will go into prison until you've proven you're not spies."

Joseph winced as he thought about what he was doing. His forehead felt warm. He kept shaking. All the old anger churned within him, yet he just wanted to know . . .

The ten men fell back and argued among themselves. "See, I told you we never should have come here," said Asher.

"We need the food," Judah retorted. "What did you expect?"

Issachar broke in. "It's because of what we did to Joseph. We've had nothing but trouble since then."

The moment Joseph heard Issachar's words, he closed his eyes, forcing back the tears. He was shaking now. Suddenly, he motioned to the guards. He instructed them to put his brothers in prison. As they were pushed forward out of the room, Judah cried, "I tell you, we're not spies."

Joseph turned and covered his face. An aide stepped forward. "My lord, are you well?"

Joseph looked up, controlling himself. "Continue selling the grain. I'll go to my room now."

In his room, he sat down on the bed and put his face in his hands. "What am I to do?" he asked out loud. No answer occurred to him.

He thought about his brothers in prison. Watching them being dragged away was such pain. And yet, something about it made him feel almost happy. Why was that?

Suddenly he said out loud, "I can do anything to them I want. Anything!"

He stood up and looked out the window. A strange mixture of anger, guilt, and joy sizzled inside him.

He clenched his fist. "No," he said, "I will love them. It is God's way."

He turned and looked out the window again. His heart settled. He knew God was with him.

Have you ever wanted to "get even"? To see that guy who cut you down burn? To see that group who mocked you knocked to pieces? We call it "sweet revenge." Why "sweet"? Perhaps because there's a certain thrill in seeing yourself vindicated and your enemies smashed.

I don't know that Joseph considered revenge as an option when his ten brothers filed up to the grain administration desk. Perhaps he was of such upright character that the thought never entered his mind.

But as I have read the story repeatedly in Genesis 37–50, I see Joseph as a man groping through a hailstorm of emotion. His schemes are so elaborate, so precise, that it appears he was wrestling with what to do with his brothers. Part of it was simply that he didn't know how to reveal himself to them without terrifying them. But part of it also was that he was struggling with his own feelings. He wanted to keep them there as long as he could. He wanted to renew family ties. He wanted to find out about his father and brother.

But don't you think there were other emotions twisting inside him—perhaps even a twinge of desire for vengeance?

There was a story in *Time* magazine (July 30, 1979) about the private "war" between Sam and John Matar. Their little duel began when John sent his brother a comic birthday greeting card. I guess it ticked Sam off, because at John's birthday the next year, Sam fired back 25 cards making fun of John for being seven years older.

Not to be outdone, John piled it on for Sam's next birthday with 50 cards teasing Sam about being overweight.

What next? Sam sent two models to sing "Happy Birthday to You" to John right in the middle of his office.

John pulled out more stops and recruited some belly dancers to sing the same song to Sam with their navels.

Next it was a plane with streamers. After that, a whole high school band. Then John sent an elephant with a banner draped over its back.

Does this sound like it was getting to be too much? Not for Sam and John. Sam arranged for a 4,000-pound "pet rock" to be dumped on John's lawn.

John trucked back ten tons of pebbles. ("The pet rock was pregnant.")

After that, Sam shipped John 4,000 pounds of manure. ("The baby rocks weren't house-trained.")

That was 1979. I'd like to hear what's happened since. I mean, where do you go from 4,000 pounds of manure?

We laugh at a story like that. But many revenge tales are not so pleasant. Consider the revenge story that's been going on between the two sons of Abraham—Ishmael and Isaac. It started 4,000 years ago and it's still going on today. The descendants of Isaac are the Jews. The descendants of Ishmael are the Arabs. For every grouping or society in our world, you can probably find an opponent, ready and thirsting for revenge.

Be that as it may, I wonder if Joseph, on seeing his brothers in Egypt to buy grain, thought about how much he'd like revenge. I wonder if he thought about putting *them* in a pit and selling them into slavery.

Yet, even if the thought did cross his mind, he never followed through with it. Rather, he displayed one of the greatest examples of forgiveness and compassion ever recorded.

What is to be our attitude toward injustices that are done to us? How are we to react when people do us wrong?

WHEN YOU'RE DONE WRONG

Remember, you *will* be done wrong in this world. People will malign you, cheat you, hate you, and wound you. And if you try to live out a Christian testimony before the world, it can get even worse. Paul wrote, "For your sake we face death all day long; we are considered as sheep to be slaughtered" (Romans 8:36). He even gives us a list of all the wrongs done to him in 2 Corinthians 11:23-27. Look at his ordeals: imprisoned, beaten, in danger of death. Five times he received thirty-nine lashes. On another occasion, Paul was stoned. It's possible that Paul actually *died* in this instance (2 Corinthians 12:1-7).

Paul knew precisely how bad it can get. He told Timothy, "In fact everyone who wants to live a godly life in Christ Jesus will be persecuted" (2 Timothy 3:12).

So you can expect as a Christian not only that things will go wrong, but that they'll go wrong deliberately because someone decided to do you in. Yet, the important thing here is how you respond to such treatment. With anger? Vengeance? Cursing? Hopelessness?

None of the above.

THREE POWERFUL THOUGHTS

There are three aspects of any situation in which you're wronged. The first is your attitude about the wrong itself. The second is your attitude toward the God who is in control of the wrong. And the third is your attitude toward the wrongdoers. On all three of these counts, Joseph performed flawlessly.

We find a complete statement of his outlook in Genesis 50:19-21. Joseph's words here are a response to his brothers shortly after Israel (Jacob), his father, died. For many years his brothers lived with the guilt of their sin against Joseph. But they had come to believe that Joseph had done nothing to them only because of their father. "He's simply waiting for Israel to die, and then he'll strike," they thought.

Finally, Israel died. Their age-old fears came to a head. What did they do? As always they resorted to trickery and deceit. They made up a story about something Israel supposedly said just before he died: "I ask you to forgive your brothers the sins and the wrongs they committed in treating you so badly" (Genesis 50:17). Joseph wept. He was still not accepted, still not loved or trusted by his brothers.

Think of it. Jacob and his sons had lived with Joseph in the land of Egypt for seventeen years. Never in all those years is it recorded that one of those ten brothers came to Joseph and personally asked forgiveness. Yet, they're willing to make up a foul lie and put it in the mouth of a dead man just to protect themselves.

This only added to the many wrongs they'd done to Joseph. Yet, Joseph, as always, remained full of mercy and understanding. He responded to their insult with kind words. "Don't be afraid. Am I in the place of God? You intended to harm me, but God intended it for good to accomplish what is now being done, the saving of many lives. So then, don't be afraid. I will provide for you and your children" (Genesis 50:19-21). In this passage we see a philosophy of life and faith that will hold anyone together despite the most trying circumstances.

THE CHRISTIAN ATTITUDE TOWARD WRONGDOING

The first thing Joseph says is, "Don't be afraid. Am I in the place of God?"

What's he talking about? Revenge. Only one person in all of creation has a right to take revenge: God. "Do not take revenge, my friends, but leave room for God's wrath, for it is written: 'It is mine to avenge; I will repay,' says the Lord" (Romans 12:19).

Why is this? Because "man's anger does not bring about the righteous life that God desires" (James 1:20). That is, no matter how justified you think you are in being angry with someone, your anger is tainted. It's fleshly, sinful, full of improper and ungodly motives. Only God can exhibit anger with perfect righteousness.

For that reason, Joseph knew he had no right to take revenge on anyone. If there was a repayment to be made, God would make it. And believe me, when

God pays someone back for his crimes, he will be paid back perfectly, justly, and absolutely. The worst any of us can do is kill the body. God can destroy soul and body in eternal hell.

So there's no need to take revenge. You can never exact a just, realistic, or complete price. If you want genuine justice, leave it in God's hand. He will repay.

But there's another reason. Ultimately, we're not even the ones sinned against; God is. Remember when David committed adultery with Bathsheba, then had Uriah, her husband, killed? When David confessed his sin, what did he say? "Please forgive me, Uriah"? No. He said to God, "Against You, You only, have I sinned and done what is evil in Your sight" (Psalm 51:4). Certainly David's sin involved others—his whole kingdom, in fact. But ultimately all sin is against God. It's His laws that are broken. It's His image that is defamed. It's His creation that is injured. It's His person that is assaulted. That's why revenge is solely His province. He has suffered the worst damage.

Thus, Joseph recognized immediately that he had no right to seek revenge on his brothers. In fact, he actually obeyed a principle that Paul referred to in Romans 12:21: "Do not be overcome by evil, but overcome evil with good." When we repay evil with evil, evil wins; all that has occurred is more evil. But when we overcome evil with good, evil loses all around. That's why the Cross was so effective. It destroyed evil on numerous fronts. First, it paid the penalty that God's justice requires from evil. Second, it made it possible for evil people to be forgiven forever. Third, it opened the way to transformation, so that evil people would cease being evil. And fourth, it accomplished all of it without resorting to evil tactics or actions.

The attitude Joseph had toward the wrongs done to

him was this: God will take care of it. As a result, he could get on with his life because he left everything in God's hands. There was no sitting around and sighing, no scheming in the dark, no wishing for disaster on the wrongdoer, no reading the obituary column to see if his enemies had finally died. Rather, it was a relaxation, a freedom from concern. "God will right every wrong and repay every sin. My job is to get on with serving and loving Him."

Do you believe that? Nahum 1:3 says, "The Lord will not leave the guilty unpunished." Leave them in His just hands. Don't take them into your own.

THE ATTITUDE TOWARD THE GOD IN CONTROL OF THE WRONGS

Joseph reveals a second element of his outlook in Genesis 50:20. Even though we may believe that God will somehow repay in the end, that's a long time to wait. We may wonder why He lets terrible things happen to us in the first place. Why doesn't He simply stop the oppressors in their boots before they get a chance to kick? Why didn't the Lord prevent Joseph's brothers from doing their foul deed? Couldn't He have intervened?

Joseph understood what happened, at least in the end. "You intended to harm me, but God intended it for good to accomplish what is now being done, the saving of many lives."

Notice two ideas here. First, the *brothers'* purpose: to do evil; to get rid of Joseph; to have revenge. Second, *God's* purpose: to do good; to provide for Jacob's family during the famine; to preserve them all.

How can there be two different purposes here, one evil and one good, when the same thing was done? It's very simple. God, being all-knowing, wise, all-powerful, good, and loving, has several distinct abilities that evil can never claim.

1. He knows everything that will ever happen. Thus, He can prepare for it from the very beginning.

2. He knows precisely how to work everything for the *best* result. His knowledge consists not merely of *what* happens, but how to make it happen the best way possible.

3. He has absolute control over everything. Nothing ever happens unless He chooses to make it happen, or He decides to allow it to happen (in the case of evil).

Thus, even though Satan or the world may try to make things go their way, ultimately God's plan is the one that's always in effect. They can do their worst, but God always has the power to make it come out best.

I don't mean "best" by our standards. God told us through Isaiah, "My thoughts are not your thoughts, neither are your ways My ways" (Isaiah 55:8). What *we* may think of as best may in no way be what *God* regards as best. Certainly, the worst crime in history was the crucifixion of Jesus Christ. Yet, even that was for good. That is, the deed itself wasn't good. But what it produced was.

Does this mean the end justifies the means? People use this idea to justify anything. They say that if what happens in the end is good, the means doesn't matter.

The problem is that God never uses evil to accomplish His ends. Rather, He sometimes lets evil have its way for the moment, while He works around it to produce a good result.

God's enemy, Satan, continually tries to foul up God's plan. He wants to destroy God. But even when Satan does his worst, God always comes in and says, "You meant it for evil, but I planned this long ago and it will actually turn out for good!"

That's why Joseph could say what he did. He saw clearly from God's perspective. His thoughts had become God's thoughts. Even with all his pain, he saw that God had done something marvelous. In that, he could rejoice.

So what about you? Can you look at your disasters as things others may mean for evil, but God means for good? If so, you have arrived at an important spiritual principle that can preserve your sanity for years to come.

THE RIGHT ATTITUDE TOWARD THE WRONGDOERS

Just the same, one can look at all this and say, "All right. I can see how Joseph might have had the right attitude toward the wrong and toward God. But what about his brothers? They had done evil. They should have been punished somehow."

Maybe so. But for Joseph to take things into his own hands, even as Prime Minister of Egypt, would have returned evil for evil. He didn't have the right to do that.

There's only one attitude to have toward people who do us wrong: forgiveness. Notice what Joseph said to his brothers. "So then, don't be afraid. I will provide for you and your children" (Genesis 50:21). He was, in effect, extending to them not only forgiveness, but also his continued loyalty, help, and love.

That's so hard. Looking someone in the eye who has brutalized you and telling them you forgive them is not easy, especially if they've hurt you deeply.

In fact, Joseph knew that. Look at a verse back in Genesis 41:51. Joseph named his firstborn son Manasseh, which means "one who causes to forget." What did he mean? He says, "God has made me forget all my trouble and all my father's household."

Take another look at that verse. What it's saying is

that Joseph—yes, even Joseph—did not have an easy time forgiving and forgetting. Manasseh was born almost twenty years after Joseph was sold into slavery by his brothers. So Joseph must have struggled for much of that time with anger and bitterness. But something had happened inside him. Scripture doesn't say what happened, but it does say, "*God* has made me forget . . . " Genuine forgiveness is impossible apart from the work and power of the Spirit. It's God alone who gives us a heart that can truly forgive.

I've seen this frequently in my own life. But one example that I always think of concerning this matter comes from the life of Corrie ten Boom. After her years in the German concentration camps of World War II, where she lost her whole family, she decided to take a message to the world. She began first in her beloved Holland. During one of her speaking engagements, she recognized a man sitting in the back of the room. He had been a cruel guard in her camp, and had even beaten her sister. Corrie felt all the old anger return. Inside, she wondered what to do. At the end of her message, she knew he would come to the door and possibly try to shake her hand. Corrie prayed for wisdom and power, but nothing happened.

When her message ended, she went to the back. Moments later, this former enemy stood before her. He obviously didn't recognize her, but he told her he'd been a guard in those camps and had done many cruel things. He said he'd become a Christian after the war and wanted to ask her forgiveness. He held out his hand.

Corrie felt revolted and sick inside. What could she do? How could she shake his hand? She prayed in her heart, "Lord, give me Your forgiveness."

Instantly, something remarkable happened inside her. God gave her grace and she sensed that yes, she could forgive. Suddenly, not only could she hold out her hand, but she could also embrace the man as a Christian brother.

Have you been done wrong? It happens to all of us. It will happen again. It may even get worse.

But there is a way to freedom and hope by having the right attitude toward the wrong itself, toward the God in control of the wrong, and toward the wrongdoer. Refuse revenge, trust God, and forgive. There's no other way, except the way to death.

Which route will you take?

5

MOSES

DEMONSTRATING YOUR LOYALTY

Aaron watched his brother Moses amble up the mountain. Momentarily, he felt relieved. *Now,* he thought, *I can get some rest.* Unfortunately, it was not to be.

As the days passed with no word from Moses, Aaron grew even wearier. All the complaints, legal cases, and arguments that Moses usually handled were now Aaron's responsibility. And the pressure never let up. There was always another case, always another interest group.

One evening, Aaron stood outside his tent rubbing his stomach after a fine meal of baked manna. He saw a large group of people moving toward him. *What now?* he thought. He turned to look for a route of escape, but it was too late. The group had already seen him.

Moments later, Lar stood before him at the head of the crowd. "We want a god who will go in front of us. This cloud we've been following is meaningless. And as for Moses, we don't know what's become of him. You're our leader now; make us a god."

Aaron was both angry and fed up. He thought of the

first and second commandments Jehovah had spoken from the mountain. **"You shall have no other gods before Me. You shall not make for yourself an idol."**

A god is what they want? he thought. *All right, then let them pay for it.*

"Get all your wives' and daughters' golden rings and jewelry and bring them here," he said. He thought that would settle the matter. After all, who would sacrifice their personal possessions to make some idol?

Two hours later, however, the people returned with six huge chests full of jewelry. Lar grinned evilly. "All you requested," he said.

Aaron stared at the gold. For a moment, he didn't know what to do. He looked up. There were thousands of people standing about, waiting.

He felt his legs go weak. *I just want to lay down and forget all this happened,* he thought.

"Well, asked Lar, "will you make us a god?"

Aaron sighed. "Build a kiln and melt the gold down."

He arranged for several of the woodcarvers to fashion a calf, seven feet high. *At least I'll make it worthy of Jehovah,* Aaron thought.

By nightfall the idol was completed—a carved wooden calf overlaid with the melted gold. Aaron stood before the people and announced that the next day there would be a feast, offerings, and appropriate ceremonies. *This may even cause everyone to worship Jehovah,* thought Aaron. *I wonder why we never thought of it before.* For a moment, he sensed an excitement.

The morning ceremonies went well. Everyone appeared reverent and pleased. The sacrifices and the feast were also successful.

But then something happened. After the feast, people began stripping and throwing their clothes into the air. Some were even having sex in the grass.

In an hour, the place was chaos—naked dancing, fornication, adultery, fistfights. The people were out of control.

Aaron looked around. Where was Moses when he was really needed?

He went into his tent and collapsed onto his bed. He stared at the ceiling of the tent, then closed his eyes and tried not to think.

Moses held the two stone tablets with the commandments etched into them. He was ready to return now. It had been forty days, and he was weary. But it was a good weariness. He felt refreshed. He was ready to lead again, to teach the people of God.

Suddenly, God spoke. His voice was hard-edged. Moses felt a terror grip him.

"Go down the mountain immediately. The people you brought out of Egypt have corrupted themselves. They've turned from the way I commanded them and have made a golden calf, worshiped it, and sacrificed to it. The leaders have told them, " 'This is your god, Israel, who brought you up from the land of Egypt.' "

Moses stood stunned. His arms went slack. One of the tablets began to slip, but he caught it.

Suddenly God spoke again, His voice like thunder, "I have seen this people, and it's clear now they are obstinate. Don't say a word to Me. I'm angry at them. I will destroy them, and I will start over. I will make of *you* a great nation."

What would you do? Here's the opportunity of a lifetime—to have God Himself make *you* the father of the greatest nation in history. All you have to do is say the word. Would you say it?

I don't want to leave you hanging, so take a look at Moses' response to God's offer in Exodus 32:11-14.

It's one of history's incredible moments, a line to remember. He said to God, "Why should Your anger burn against Your people, whom You brought up out of Egypt with great power and a mighty hand?

"Why should the Egyptians say, 'It was with evil intent that He brought them out, to kill them in the mountains and to wipe them off the face of the earth'? Turn from Your fierce anger; relent and do not bring disaster on Your people. Remember your servants Abraham, Isaac, and Israel, to whom You swore by Your own self: 'I will make your descendants as numerous as the stars in the sky and I will give your descendants all this land I promised them and it will be their inheritance forever.' "

What a perfect response. It's precisely how a godly leader should respond when faced with the choice of staying with or leaving his people. It's an expression of intense loyalty (a loyalty Moses didn't always have).

Could you be that loyal?

WHAT IS LOYALTY?

When Adolph Hitler became chancellor of Germany, millions vowed their loyalty to him. Loyalty became such a mark of his government that people stopped greeting one another with "Hello." Instead, they raised their arms in salute, clicked their heels together, and said, "Heil, Hitler." Many of those people died out of loyalty for the man.

The Ayatollah Khomeini in Iran commands absolute loyalty. Terrorists drive bomb-laden trucks into American barracks and explode them, killing themselves in the process. But is this the loyalty that Scripture speaks of? Of course not.

Jesus summarized Christian loyalty in Matthew 10:37-39. He said, "Anyone who loves his father or mother more than Me is not worthy of Me; anyone who loves his son or daughter more than Me is not worthy of Me; and anyone who does not take his cross and follow Me is not worthy of Me. Whoever finds his life will lose it, and whoever loses his life for My sake will find it."

James said it another way. "Anyone who chooses to be a friend of the world becomes an enemy of God" (James 4:4).

John said, "If anyone loves the world, the love of the Father is not in him" (1 John 2:15).

And then there's Jesus' ultimate statement in Luke 14:26: "If anyone comes to Me and does not hate his father and mother, his wife and children, his brothers and sisters—yes, even his own life—he cannot be My disciple." Jesus pictures such a level of commitment and love for Him that, in comparison, all other relationships look like hate. It's not that He literally wants us to hate those people; but that our love and loyalty to Him should go far beyond anything we have for people in this world.

What then is loyalty? I'd define it this way: loving Jesus and all that He stands for so much that no one in this world could keep you from obeying Him. Loyalty results in love, obedience, endurance, and faith in any and every situation of life.

MOSES' SITUATION

Look again at Moses' situation. It *appears* that God Himself was having a temper tantrum. God begins by saying, "Go down, because *your* people, whom *you* brought up out of Egypt." They were Moses' people? Moses brought them up from Egypt?

After that, God tells Moses, "Now leave Me alone so that My anger may burn against them and that I may destroy them." God is saying, "Don't bother Me now, Moses, I'm hot. Don't try to talk Me out of it."

Finally, He says, "I will make you into a great nation." In other words, "Just let Me at these people and I'll make you a nation in their place." Moses' prayer in the following verses looks like a friend holding back an angry person from a fight.

What is happening here? Has God Himself gone berserk?

I think not. I'm convinced that what we have here is an absolutely unique situation. Moses was the leader of a horde of stubborn rebels. Repeatedly they challenged, mocked, and turned on God.

Yet, this was only the beginning. Moses would be leading these people for the next forty years. God needed to know if Moses would remain loyal even in the face of the greatest provocation or opportunity. I don't mean that God didn't know that already. He is omniscient. But because *we* live in time, and because we change in the course of time, He had to test Moses. Thus, He Himself forced the confrontation. It was as though God said, "OK, Moses, I'm going to offer you the greatest opportunity any man could have. You know who I am, what I have called you to, and what My purposes are. I want to see if you'll desert your people when you have what some might consider a golden opportunity."

Do you see the point? Anyone who wants to lead others, or even be a part of a team—anyone who wants to serve God—must pass this test. Will *you* be loyal to God and His program no matter what other opportunities come your way?

AN IMPORTANT TEST

In this world, multitudes of opportunities will arise. Money, sex, popularity, prizes, awards—all sorts of things will beckon to us. They'll say, "Come on, forget this Christianity thing and come with me. I'll show you what really matters." They'll demand that you compromise.

God was offering Moses something that leaders everywhere are offered: a chance to attain personal goals instead of God's program and plans. In other words, before Moses could lead Israel, an important problem had to be solved: whom would he be loyal to—God or himself?

Moses passed the test. I'm certain he had no idea why God was acting the way He was. He may have felt astonished and dismayed. But he had to take the position of mediator between God and the people of Israel. In reality, he was being tested about all he knew of God and His plans.

Abraham passed the same test. When he helped the king of Sodom in Genesis 14, the king offered to give Abraham everything. It would have made him rich instantly. But Abraham said no. He had sworn to God that he wouldn't take anything because the king might say *he* had made Abraham rich. And Abraham would not have that said of anyone but God (Genesis 14:22-24).

David experienced a similar test. Remember when he and his men were hiding in the cave and King Saul came in to relieve himself? What did David's men say? "Now's your chance, David. Kill him." But David refused. He said, "The Lord forbid that I should do such a thing to my master, the Lord's anointed" (1 Samuel 24:6).

This was God's test. God was saying, "Will you, David, remain faithful to what you know of My Word and character, even in the midst of a ripe opportunity?" David said, "I will."

There were many others who didn't do quite so well. In fact, they flunked the test: Cain, Samson, Judas Iscariot, even Peter at one point.

In Galatians 2, Paul relates how he confronted Peter about hypocrisy. Peter had come to Antioch and participated in everything the Gentile Christians were doing. But one day, some Jews from James, the leader in Jerusalem, came by. Suddenly, Peter choked. Jew-Gentile relations within the church were still a touchy matter. Some Jews believed they shouldn't eat with Gentiles, even though the Gentiles were born again. Apparently this was the case with James' men. Peter began to withdraw from the Gentiles. Then all the Jews did. And finally, Paul's best friend, Barnabas did. So Paul confronted Peter about his hypocrisy. In that situation, Peter failed the test, if only momentarily.

Moses, later in life, would also fail such a test. In Numbers 20, the people murmured about the lack of water. God ordered Moses to speak to a large rock in the area, and He would cause water to pour out. But Moses was angry. Instead of speaking to the rock, he struck it twice with his staff, and made it look like he himself had performed the miracle instead of God. He failed an important test. For that, God disciplined him by refusing to allow him to go into the land of Canaan with the people. He would die beforehand. Such is the seriousness of obeying God and being faithful to His Word.

BECOMING A LOYAL PERSON

How then do you become one who is faithful, loyal, and trustworthy in the eyes of God?

First, *by knowing God.*

When God became enraged and threatened to destroy Israel and make of Moses a new nation, I'm certain it astonished Moses. God was acting unlike any way Moses had ever seen.

In the same way, there are many circumstances which befall Christians that we don't understand.

Worse, we can't seem to square them with the character of God. For instance, in our area, a group of local students celebrated their junior prom. Everything was done right. They had chaperones, stuck to the rules, even had a designated driver for their van. But the driver made a mistake. She went through a blinking red light. Another car came through with the right of way and crashed into them. One young man, a church-goer and all-around good guy, was killed. What's the first thing we say to such a tragedy? "Why did you let this happen, God?"

Moses might have thought that in his situation. "How could you let the people get out of control like this, God?"

But more importantly, when God erupted with anger, Moses might have said, "How can you be acting like this, God?"

What's the answer? Revelation—the truth about God. What precisely *does* Scripture reveal about God's nature and person? Two chapters later, Moses would receive a special vision of God. In that vision, God would say, "The Lord, the Lord, the compassionate and gracious God, slow to anger, abounding in love and faithfulness" (Exodus 34:6). How does that revelation square with how God was acting back in Exodus 32?

It doesn't. That's why knowing God is so critical to faithfulness. If you don't know the facts He's revealed about Himself, you'll desert Him in the crunch. Too many things in life will drive you away from Him.

There are many things we assume about God's nature that lead us to believe error. Things like:

- God is love; therefore, He would never judge anyone.
- God is gracious; therefore, He will eventually save everyone.

- God is just; therefore, I should never have to put up with injustice.
- God is all-powerful; therefore, nothing bad should ever happen to me.

Our wrong conclusions about His nature lead to faithlessness. In the Parable of the Sower (Matthew 13:1-9), the second soil received the word with joy, but it was shallow and, though the seed sprang up, it had no root. When the sun came out, it withered. That's the essence of disloyalty. If you have no root—if you don't know what Scripture says God is like, you'll make all sorts of wrong judgments and assumptions about life. Eventually, being a Christian will look like the ultimate foolishness.

When God said He'd destroy Israel, Moses made a spontaneous, but biblical response. He said, "The Egyptians would have a heyday with that, Lord! They'd say you brought us out here to kill us. And that just simply doesn't make sense considering who You are!"

Moses couldn't have understood that God was testing him. What he did understand was that God's actions weren't true to His revealed character. But the only way Moses could know God's revealed character was through knowing God. In order to cope with and explain the problems of life biblically, we must know God personally through Jesus, or we'll come to all the wrong conclusions.

King David wrote in Psalm 34:8: "Taste and see that the Lord is good; blessed is the man who takes refuge in Him." You get to know God by learning of Jesus Christ. Like Jesus said, "Take My yoke upon you and learn from Me, for I am gentle and humble in heart, and you will find rest for your souls" (Matthew 11:29). By learning of Jesus and discovering His true nature and person, you'll love Him more day by day.

You'll begin to understand why life happens as it does. And you'll trust Him for the things you don't understand.

Second, we become loyal to God *by understanding His plans and principles.*

It's possible to know God and still fail to understand where He's going. But when we do know where He's headed, we also know what to expect when we get there.

When God offered to make of Moses a great nation, Moses instantly thought of God's revealed plans. What God was saying contradicted every known promise He'd ever made. So Moses responded, "Remember your servants Abraham, Isaac and Israel, to whom You swore by Your own self: 'I will make your descendants as numerous as the stars in the sky and I will give your descendants all this land I promised them, and it will be their inheritance'" (Exodus 32:13). Moses passed the test because he knew God's revealed purposes and plans. When something contradicted them, he knew instantly what to say and do.

Third, we become faithful *by knowing God's heart.*

I suspect that in the midst of God's outburst, Moses was wondering something that he hardly dared to mention: "Is this how God *really* feels?" But he came to the conclusion, "No. I know the God who is loving, kind, and compassionate. So this must be something else."

Moses knew God's heart. And knowing God's heart will, beyond anything else, keep a person loyal.

Paul wrote to Timothy, "That is why I am suffering as I am. Yet I am not ashamed, because I know whom I have believed, and am convinced that He is able to guard what I have entrusted to Him for that day" (2 Timothy 1:12). Paul endured whippings, beatings, shipwrecks, hatred, malice, slander, and every other form of persecution for one reason: He knew God's heart. For that reason, he loved Jesus and could never desert Him. He obeyed to the point of death.

Jesus wants us to know His heart. "Here I am! I stand at the door and knock. If anyone hears My voice and opens the door, I will come in and eat with Him, and He with Me" (Revelation 3:20). "God demonstrates His own love for us in this: While we were still sinners, Christ died for us" (Romans 5:8). "I have loved you with an everlasting love" (Jeremiah 31:3).

When a vast throng of followers deserted Jesus in John 6, He turned to His twelve disciples and asked them if they wanted to leave too. Peter answered, "Lord, to whom shall we go? You have the words of eternal life. We believe and know that You are the Holy One of God" (John 6:68-69).

Thomas was so committed that when Jesus proposed going into enemy territory to see Lazarus just a few days after the Jews had threatened to kill Him, he said, "Let us also go, that we may die with Him" (John 11:16).

Tradition tells us that when it was time for Peter to die, he refused to be crucified like Jesus was. He felt he wasn't worthy. So he was crucified upside down.

What was it that drove these men, that forced them to cling so tenaciously to Jesus? It was more than words, more than miracles, more than personal friendship. It was His heart. He loved them. And they knew it. They were drawn to that love like thirst-crazed men to an oasis.

WHAT HOLDS YOU?

What then is it that holds you?

If you do not know Him and His Word, if you have not experienced His heart, you have limits. And you'll choke.

But if you know Him, if you've been awakened to His heart, then nothing in this world can stop you.

In the early days of Christianity, Nero opposed the faith vehemently. Some Christians were thrown to the lions in the arena while the Roman multitudes watched. Frequently, Nero strung Christians up on stakes at his garden parties. They were then set on fire. He put them in the skins of wild animals, then hunted them with dogs who tore them to pieces.

But there was one thing the persecutors never understood. As the lions charged out of their cages in the arena, as the flames were lit, as the dogs bit into their flesh, these Christians often did a strange and marvelous thing—they sang.

Scientists tell us an unusual fact about singing: you cannot do it if you are afraid. Fear causes the throat to constrict. Sounds will not come out.

What was it that possessed these Christians, that made them able to sing—even in the face of death?

The heart of Christ.

6

NATHAN

CONFRONTING THE LEADER

Nathan slumped deeper in his seat. "It can't be," he muttered. "Why, I thought . . . " His voice trailed off.

His mind raced through the events of the previous year: the strange episode of David staying home from battle; the sudden death of Uriah in the *front* of the battle, where a captain normally wouldn't be; David bringing Bathsheba, Uriah's widow, into his own house; the big speech; Bathsheba, shy and coy, not speaking; David exhorting his family to accept her as his wife.

Then the child.

The timing of the birth had been odd. The child was born precisely nine months after Uriah died. But Nathan thought it must be a coincidence. He told himself not to worry. David was a righteous man, a man who feared Jehovah. Why, only a few years before, David had wanted to build a temple for the Lord to dwell in. He was the most zealous believer in the kingdom.

"How can it be?" he asked.

But the revelation had been direct, stark, and searing. God had spoken to him as never before, never quite so clearly.

"Over a year," Nathan murmured, "he's had over a year to repent of this deed. Why, he's even written psalms for the worship." Nathan paused. "Or has he?"

He thought back over the past year's worship services David had attended. There had been the usual singing. But there was something else, something he'd noticed—a distance, maybe. David wouldn't look him in the eye. Perhaps that was it. And there hadn't been any new psalms, not even a bit of poetry.

"I should have known," he said. "I should have seen it. How could I, of everyone in the kingdom, have been so blind?"

He stood up and pounded his fist on the table. "It must be confronted. I cannot leave him in this condition. And if necessary . . . "

Nathan thought about the dictates of the law. For an adulterer, there was only one punishment: stoning. No mercy, no offer of hope unless God Himself granted it.

Nathan sat down and sighed. "Now how am I to do this?" he wondered. "David is a volatile man. I could easily provoke him into further sins if I don't take the right approach."

He didn't want to attack the king. He wanted to restore him to proper fellowship. It would have to be done gently, yet directly. Timing was of utmost importance. Yet he had to do it soon. He couldn't dawdle about it. David had been in this sinful condition long enough.

Nathan considered a number of approaches. A public denunciation perhaps? There were many prophets who had taken that route with sin. Just march into the market and start shouting about it.

Nathan shook his head. "That wouldn't be fair," he said. "It's not public knowledge. Furthermore, he's my friend."

He considered sending a servant with a letter.

"No, I must do it personally. I won't be branded a coward."

He decided he would speak to David in private.

"Now what words will I use?"

He closed his eyes and thought. Several times he stopped and prayed. He thought about the things David loved. Suddenly it struck him. "A lamb!" he said. "David's special love and compassion for sheep, for the broken, the hurting."

Nathan considered several possibilities, but finally he hit upon a story, a little parable he would tell. He wasn't sure if it was the best approach, but he knew he needed to get to David's heart first and fast.

The moment Ablijah, the king's servant, let him in, Nathan trembled. Twice he thought about going back, but decided against it. He was determined.

When he was led into the throne room, King David looked up with direct, tired eyes. "You've asked for a conference?"

Nathan nodded, then took a deep breath. His heart drummed in his chest. He launched into a story about a poor man who had one lamb that he loved and treated as a child. A rich man took the lamb, slaughtered it, and fed it to some of his visitors, even though he had hundreds of such lambs himself.

David's eyes grew wide. He was furious. "As the Lord lives, the man who has done this deserves to die!"

Nathan trembled. He held up his hand and pointed. He felt himself filling with the power of God. "You are the man!" he shouted.

David stared at him.

"Thus says the Lord God of Israel. 'It is I who anointed you king over Israel. It is I who delivered you from Saul. I gave you your master's house and his wives into your care. I gave you all Israel and Judah. And if that had been too little, I would have added many more such things to these.' "

David slumped and his chin fell.

Nathan went on. "Why have you despised God's Word by doing evil in His sight? You struck down Uriah the Hittite with the sword, and took his wife to be your wife."

Nathan watched David's face. David looked up, his face contorted with pain.

" 'Now,' " shouted Nathan, " 'the sword will never depart from your house. I will raise up evil against you from your own household. I will even take your wives from before your eyes and give them to your companion, and he shall lie with them in broad daylight. *You* did it in secret. But *I* will do this before all Israel.' "

Nathan stopped speaking abruptly and waited. His heart jumped within him. He wondered if the king would repent, or lie, or make an excuse or . . .

Tears came into David's eyes. He put his face in his hands. "I have sinned," he murmured.

Nathan sighed. "The Lord has taken away your sin. You shall not die."

David looked up, shielding his eyes with his hand.

"However . . . " Nathan held up his hand. "Because you have given the enemies of the Lord an opportunity to blaspheme His name, the child of the woman will die."

David slumped again into his throne as though he'd been struck. He looked up at Nathan with pleading eyes.

Nathan turned and walked toward the door. He hoped David wouldn't ask him anything more. But his anger was gone. He knew David was back on the path.

Confrontation. Have you ever faced one? It's not easy. No one likes a confrontation. Anyone who does is probably a fool or a bully. Yet, confronting Christians about their sin is one of the essential elements of Christian living. Leviticus 19:17 even tells us that failing to confront a sinner is the same as hating him. What kind of person would pass a burning house and not say a word? Who would let a four-year-old play with a cobra? To see a person commit sin, especially a brother in Christ, and say nothing, is the same thing.

Let's remember at the start that even though the word "confrontation" conjures up many poisonous images in our minds, it's not meant to be that way. The idea of a "face-to-face confrontation" with someone gives most of us the shakes. Often, when I'm in a situation that requires speaking the truth in love, I hyperventilate, imagine all sorts of horrid responses, and try to find any way to avoid saying what I need to say. But a confrontation needn't be a horror show. It can be done with kindness, understanding, and in such a way that both parties feel energized and loved as people.

THE IMPORTANCE OF CONFRONTING

Why is confrontation so critical?

There are a number of scriptural reasons for speaking the truth to erring Christians. First, to maintain the purity of the church in the eyes of God and the world.

One of the strongest examples of confrontation in the Bible is found in 1 Corinthians 5. In this passage, Paul spoke of expelling a sinning Christian from the church fellowship because he was sleeping with his father's wife. The Corinthians had failed to deal with the sinner. Some friends mentioned it to Paul when they visited him in Ephesus, and he took action. In verse 6 he reminds the Corinthians, "Don't you know that a little yeast works through the whole batch of dough?" What happens to a batch of scrambled eggs when you mix in one rotten egg? The whole batch goes bad. What happens to the church when a Christian sins and no one does anything about it? The whole batch is affected. The influence spreads. More people get involved in the sin.

What's more, in the eyes of the world, the church looks like a group of fools and hypocrites if they tolerate sin. Unbelievers say things like, "Christians are no different than anyone else, so where do they get off claiming to be God's children?" And, "They're all a bunch of fakes." And, "They talk big, but live just like everyone else." The church ends up with no testimony. Its spiritual power is stunted. Its message is written off. Its principles are scoffed at. Worst of all, its Lord is mocked.

At a more personal level, we cannot tolerate sin because we're actually "members of one body" (Ephesians 4:25). That means all Christians are connected. We're Christ's body. Have you ever burned your hand on a hot stove? When your hand was there, touching the stove, did your brain say, "Aw, I don't care about that hand because I'm the brain—let it burn"? No way. Your brain recognizes that that hand is part of your body. Therefore, it tells the arm to jerk away quickly before the hand gets hurt.

Every Christian is a part of the same body. To fail to tell a sinning brother that he's hurting himself—and the body—is to sabotage your own body. It's like using your right hand to chop off your left pinky finger.

Second, confrontation is critical because we all have blind spots. We can't see them on our own. We *need* to be told that we're sinning.

Jeremiah said our hearts are deceitful. They lie to

us. When we sin, we tell ourselves, "No one knows." Or, "It's such a little thing; it really doesn't matter." Or, "Maybe it's wrong, but I'm not really sure, so I'll go ahead and do it anyway." Or, "God understands why I have to do this." We lie to ourselves, rationalize, and find good reasons for doing bad things.

But if someone steps in and says, "Hey, that's wrong!" we often wake up—fast.

Third, confronting sin is critical not only because it's corrective, but because it's preventative as well. James said it this way: "If one of you should wander from the truth and someone should bring him back, remember this: whoever turns a sinner from the error of his way will save him from death and cover over a multitude of sins" (James 5:19-20).

What does James mean by saying it will "save him from death" and "cover over a multitude of sins"?

This isn't speaking necessarily about salvation (although that's true if the sinner isn't a Christian). Instead, this passage is saying that the sinning Christian will be saved from broken fellowship with God, which is a living death. When we sin and fail to confess it, a spiritual, mental, and emotional wall goes up between us and God. We feel joyless, loveless, without peace. Why? Because those realities come only from God's Spirit. We cannot experience them if we're disobeying and rebelling against Him. All we feel is empty, guilty, and rejected. That's death. When we turn a sinning brother back and move him to confess his sin, the wall goes down. He and the Lord embrace and walk together again in harmony.

Turning such a person back also "covers over a multitude of sins." James means not only that we'll prevent him from sinning more, but that all his past sins will be hidden from sight as well. People will forgive and forget. Relationships will heal.

Think of Paul on the Damascus Road. He was heading to Damascus to cast more Christians into prison. But what happened? Jesus Himself stopped him. He turned Paul from the error of his way. How many sins do you suppose were prevented by that act?

Fourth, confrontation is critical because it helps us grow. "As iron sharpens iron, so one man sharpens another" (Proverbs 27:17). You can't sharpen a knife with cotton balls or whipped cream. You sharpen it by rubbing it against an equally strong and hard substance.

That's confrontation—speaking the truth, which is the hardest and strongest substance in the world. It cuts. It chips. It sharpens. In the hands of a loving person, it has the power to make a man sharp, beautiful, and useful.

God uses people. He's not going to write the message in the sky, "Mark, you need to straighten up!" No, He'll send some bold soul to speak the truth to me. It's not always comfortable. Transformation never is. But He'll use it to change me.

One day I picked up a little nine-year-old girl named Jan to drive her to a local "haunted house" on Halloween. As we drove along, we came to a traffic light. A hundred feet before I reached it, it turned yellow. Since I was already late, I decided to go through. It turned red just as I reached it.

I hoped Jan wouldn't notice, but just as I got past the light, she moaned and said, "Uh oh, guess what you just did."

I played dumb. "What?" I asked innocently.

"You went through a red light."

"Well, actually it wasn't a red light, Jan," I explained. "You see, it was yellow, and—"

"It sure looked red to me!"

I decided not to argue further. We went on and I

figured she'd forgotten it.

Then it happened again, almost identically. I ran another yellow/red light.

Immediately, she piped up, "Guess what—you did it again!"

I felt angry now. "Jan, you're allowed to go through when it's yellow."

"But it was red."

I tried to explain again about traffic regulations.

She said, "Well, I know a red light when I see one!"

It was a hopeless case.

So what happened when we arrived at a second house to pick up two more kids? Jan exclaimed, "Guess what Mark did—two times?"

Ever wish you could crawl under the floor mats?

That's just one case. But that little girl's zesty words spoke to my heart. It was a small step toward a long reform. In my life there have been a multitude of such little truth-speaks. Sometimes they've been comical; occasionally they've been harsh. But all have been redemptive.

HOW TO CONFRONT AN ERRING CHRISTIAN

Nathan's confrontation with David in 2 Samuel 12 provides several of the important principles we need to use in speaking the truth to sinning Christians. But let's ask an important question at the start: What is to be my attitude when I go to confront someone? Glee? "Now I've got him right where I want him." Superiority? "I've come down from the heights with a message from the King of kings." Anger? "You slimeball, you deserve to be smashed for this kind of conduct." Fear? "You won't hit me if I say this, will you?"

None of the above.

We should have only one attitude: love. Remember, we speak the truth in *love*. That means our purpose is restoration, to bring people back into harmony with God's plan and Word. We care. We don't want to see them destroy themselves, break friendships, or ruin others' lives. We want to help, to "set the broken bone," to see them live in the power and joy of the Spirit.

I have been in some severe confrontations. There were harsh words. At times, I've been angry, nasty, condescending, superior, even happy at the thought of popping someone else's balloon. But it was all wrong. Even though we often fail, we're always to strive for that gentle spirit of love.

NATHAN'S ACTIONS

Notice several facts about the circumstances of Nathan's actions.

1. He went because *God sent him.*

Note that. God's means is people. Not a message in the sky, but people going to people. The Lord likes to dress up His severe words in the satin of flesh. He doesn't strike you down and leave you broken and bleeding on the side of the road. No, He sends a person, very much like yourself, and has him speak.

2. Nathan went *personally.*

How many of us would rather write an anonymous letter? Or better yet, talk someone else into "dropping a hint"? But that wasn't Nathan's way or God's way. Nathan went personally. He said it to David's face.

3. Nathan went *privately.*

Although Scripture is not completely clear about the time or place of the confrontation, it does appear to be private. Nathan didn't stand up during worship and offer a seething denunciation of David to the congregation, nor did he piously offer a request in a prayer meeting that "the Lord would help David repent of his adultery and murder."

Jesus reasserts this principle in Matthew 18:15. "If your brother sins against you, go and show him his fault, just between the two of you." That's crucial. No one likes his or her faults shouted from the rooftops or over the phone lines. Confront people in a private place where they feel secure.

4. Nathan went *immediately*.

There's no procrastination here. He went as soon as he was aware of the problem. That's especially tough. We like to think that with time "it'll go away." Or we hope someone else will tell them. Or we reason that "they'll get it on their own." That's not scriptural. Go as soon as you know. Don't wait. Waiting will only make you more nervous about confronting, and the sinner more hardened in his or her sin and deceit.

5. Nathan went *confidently*.

One of the most difficult things about confrontation is that you never know what kind of response you will get. Anger? Hatred? Rejection? An argument? A firing squad? Remember, Satan can put all those images in your mind and make you afraid to go.

Nathan didn't know what David would do. But he had confidence in God, that the Lord was in charge and would work all things for good.

There is one more aspect of confrontation that is not directly evident in this story.

6. Go with a *willingness to listen*.

Remember, there's always the possibility you've misinterpreted certain actions. Give the one you're confronting a chance to offer an explanation. Maybe there is a genuine alternative. Maybe it's not sin, but merely a conflict of opinions or a misreading of the facts. Give him a chance to tell *his* side of the story. (In Nathan's case, of course, he'd received his information by revelation, so there was no mistake about the details.)

NATHAN'S WORDS

We can learn not only from what Nathan *did,* but what he *said* as well. Let's examine some principles found in Nathan's words to David.

First, *be sure of your facts.* What if you run up against a situation where the person you confront begins making all sorts of excuses and rationalizations? What do you do then? The first thing to do is to make sure of your facts. If the sin was against you, or in your presence, then you're an eyewitness. There can be no question. But to bring off an effective speaking of the truth, you must know whereof you speak. Don't go in with what you think is a loaded gun, only to discover you've got nothing but blanks. You'll not only look like a fool, but it could prevent a real restoration and make things worse.

It is also important to deal only with the facts. Stay away from opinions, hearsay, and so on. Facts are facts. Either it happened or it didn't. Either it's a sin or it isn't. Don't let yourself get hung up in the gray areas because you didn't have the facts straight.

Second, *remember that timing and approach are important.* Notice how Nathan came to David: with a heartrending parable. That doesn't mean that every time you confront someone, you need to come up with some tearjerker story to lead it off. Rather, it means that Nathan was acutely aware that simply stomping on David for his sin wasn't the proper approach. He needed to appeal to David to help him see his error.

When you go to confront someone, always consider timing and approach. How will you say what you have to say? What words will you begin with? Is there something you can say that will put the person at ease and convey that you care? When is the best time to do it? Will your coming be regarded as an intrusion, thus making your words less palatable?

I'm not saying you need to sugarcoat your words, or hedge, or compromise, or give in. I'm saying that you should take the time to prepare yourself and the sinner appropriately.

Third, *use the Word of God as the basis for your claims.* Who are *we* to tell anyone they've sinned? Good question.

But when we use God's Word, we're not going with *our* opinions, traditions, ideas, or preferences. We're showing what God says on the subject. If they reject that, they're not rejecting us, but God and His Word. That's far more serious.

I recall a vigorous confrontation I had with a sharp, successful businessman who intimidated me continually. Because of his conduct in certain church meetings, I had to confront him. When I did, he tried every trick he could to slide out of the situation. At one point, it appeared that it was his opinion against mine. I was stymied. But suddenly, I thought of a Scripture verse. I opened my Bible and read it. The discussion ended immediately. He was dead silent. He couldn't argue with Scripture because he claimed to be a leader who believed in that very Word.

Fourth, *give the person a chance to answer and repent, if necessary.* Notice that Nathan gave his say in verses 7-12 and then simply stopped. I have made the mistake of feeling uncomfortable in silence, so I've just gone on talking. That was wrong of me.

We should stop when we've had our say. If there's silence, let it be. Wait. Give the person a chance to think, to answer, to repent. Silence means the mind is working, that something's sinking in. Don't disturb that process with verbal junk.

That's hard. We usually want to make a special effort to assure, to offer love, to extend a hand. But we need to give God time to work.

Fifth, *if the person repents, remind him that God forgives.*

When David repented, Nathan extended to him God's forgiveness. Sometimes we forget this. We want the person to feel it down deep, to realize how much they've hurt us—to make them sweat just a little. But that's not God's way. The repentant sinner receives instant and eternal forgiveness. That's tremendous, isn't it? Isn't that how *we'd* like to be treated? That's God's way.

Sixth, and finally, *you should remind the person that, though he's forgiven, there may be consequences for his sin.* Nathan spelled out to David several terrible things that would befall him as a result of his sin, the first being that Bathsheba's son would die. Isn't that a bit scary? What kind of forgiveness is that?

Precisely the kind God offers. His forgiveness is of an eternal nature. As far as judgment and any kind of eternal penalty for sin, it's all gone. That sin will never be brought up here or in the hereafter.

However, because the sin was committed in time and space, there may be consequences in time and space. The sinner may suffer pain, rejection, heartache, or a personal limitation as a result of what he's done. God will not rearrange history just to make sure nothing bad happens to you. Sometimes He does lift the consequences. A person does something wrong, he repents, and the sin is gone. He lives happily ever after. But more frequently, there are consequences. Chuck Colson still went to jail despite his confessions in the Watergate affair. Johnny Cash's family still suffered emotional damage from his alcoholism, even though he repented. And any sin we commit today may affect us for the rest of our lives, even though we'll never have to pay for it in eternity.

Is that fair? Sure. When we sin, it affects the whole

world. We've set in motion forces that God chooses not to stop most of the time. It's like throwing a pebble into a lake. We may extract the pebble, but the waves are still there.

So where do you find yourself? Are you aware of a Christian who is committing sin? Do you care about him? Do you love him?

Then act. Speak the truth in love. It may save his life, and yours.

7

RAHAB THE HARLOT

IF I DON'T DO IT, NOBODY WILL

"They'll soon reach the Jordan," said Gliam. "I watched them from the hills. What do you think they'll do, Mother?" Gliam gazed at his mother as she prepared raisin cakes at the table. "Do you think they'll take Jericho?"

Rahab glanced at him and shuddered. "I think there's no stopping them. They have the power of God, the real God."

"The real God? Who's that?"

Rahab sighed. "I'm not sure who the real God is. But I am sure it's not Baal or Asherah, or any of the others in the city. They do nothing."

Gliam shook his head. "Mother, you'll be brought before the authorities if you keep talking like that."

"The authorities have more pressing matters to attend to than the heresy trial of a prostitute."

"You mean the invaders?" Gliam asked.

"Yes," Rahab answered, "that's why they've been meeting in town every night—to figure out what to do."

"I think we should gather our army together and

defeat the Hebrews."

"Have you seen them moving through the hills?" Rahab asked. "There are thousands of them, perhaps millions; more people than I've ever seen. They walk right along like they own everything."

"They'll never take Jericho," Gliam said emphatically. "Our walls are the best and our warriors are the best. Who do they think they are?"

"The people of God," murmured Rahab.

"Come on, Mother. Baal is our god. He'll protect us."

"Just like he protected the Midianites?" Rahab asked.

Gliam looked down at his plate. That *had* bothered him. Everyone had said that the Hebrews would get no further than Midian. Five kings joined forces to stop them there. And what had happened? All five of them died. But it had to be a fluke. Something had gone wrong. Surely they couldn't take Jericho.

"You're not afraid, are you, Mother?" He paused and waited. "Mother?"

"Yes, I'm afraid," she said quietly. "We can't stop them. The real God is with them. No one can stop Him."

"Why do think the real God has chosen them?" Gliam asked.

Rahab shivered in the cool night air. "I don't know, but I plan to find out."

"Find out? How?"

"Talk to them."

"They'll kill you."

"I'm not so sure about that."

She went back to her raisin cakes. "I saw two of them today," she said quietly.

Gliam jumped up. "Where? They should be killed."

"In the market. Now hush. Someone may hear."

"In the market? How could they do that?"

"I think they were spies. If I see them tomorrow, I'll speak to them. I have to know."

"Know what?"

"Who their God is."

"Why?"

"Because I want to know Him."

Gliam swallowed and sat down slowly. "You mean you'd help them?"

"Absolutely."

"The king would have you executed."

"Better to be dead in the hands of the real God than alive in this death pit."

"Do you really think that this is the end?"

"Yes." She put the raisin cakes on a tray to take up to the roof. Suddenly, she faced Gliam and looked hard into his eyes. "Someday, Gliam, you will understand. I've lived my whole life as a harlot. I want something better. I want a home where I have love and respect. I want more than what Baal offers, or Asherah. All they do is demand. 'Do this.' 'Do that.' 'Appease me.' I hate it. I want to know the truth. All my life I've wanted it. And I'm convinced this is my chance—and your chance too, Gliam. We'd better take it."

When she finished, she gazed at him, then blinked and turned away. He watched her go out the door to the outside stairway. Suddenly he knew that he'd help her. *If I see a Hebrew,* he thought, *I'll invite him to come over.*

Almost every day each one of us is confronted with a situation where we're asked to help, to lend a hand, to give of ourselves. Most of the time it's no trouble. But then there are those occasions . . .

● What if, while driving, you saw a weird-looking person in a wild outfit hitchhiking? How seriously would you consider giving him a ride?

• What if a man came to your door at night saying something about a flat tire and asking to use your phone? Would you let him in?

• What if you got a phone call at 2 A.M. and someone strange on the other end asked you for counsel? What would your reaction be?

• What if you walked into the lunchroom and spotted two seats left at your usual table—one next to a friend, and the other next to the local nerd? Which one would you take?

REFUSING TO HELP

Too often people refuse to help others in need. Some time ago, I read of a woman in New York who was raped on a back street while people watched it from their open windows. No one even called the police!

I'm sure you've read about muggings, murders, and other criminal acts where witnesses "didn't want to get involved," so they refused to testify at the trial. Don't those people outrage you?

Why do these things happen? Why do people simply refuse to help? There are many reasons. Laziness is one. They just don't want to pull themselves up out of the easy chair.

Another reason is the cost of helping. They might have to give money, time, or energy. Many people aren't willing to sacrifice those things for total strangers.

A third reason is that many people just don't care. Jesus said that in the last days, "the love of most will grow cold" (Matthew 24:12). Isn't that precisely what we see today—the love of many "grown cold"?

A fourth reason is that some people have been burned by con artists pretending to be in need of help, but who are really seeking a handout at another's expense. That type of thing can make you skeptical of even genuinely needy people.

A fifth reason, strangely, is both philosophical and theological. Remember Jesus' story of the Good Samaritan? A priest and a Levite both neglected to help the robbed and beaten man. Why? According to certain laws which they interpreted in certain ways, they didn't want to become ceremonially unclean by touching blood or a dead man. Their rituals came before anything else.

Of course, Jesus condemned them for such interpretations of God's Law. But it still happens today. In India, while everything from ants to cattle have a feast, people starve. Why? Because the Indian religion, Hindusim, believes in a Law of Karma which says people starve because they deserve it, so we shouldn't help them. But cattle must have the food because they're sacred.

Other people today have a philosophy of life that says, "Look out for number one," "Only the fittest survive," and "Nice guys finish last." Jesus is even thought of as the "nice guy" who got crucified. Therefore, you shouldn't be a nice guy under any circumstances. "Do unto others *before* they do unto you."

A DIFFERENT KIND OF HELP

But Rahab thought remarkably differently from these people. She faced a situation that was unique, and she still helped. Consider her circumstances:

1. Being a harlot (prostitute) was certainly a questionable occupation. She'd have been an easy target for someone's revenge.

2. Many people in town probably considered her presence a nuisance. They would have taken advantage of any chance to throw her out.

3. The oncoming nation of Hebrews provoked great fear among the people of Jericho. Anyone assisting them would have immediately suffered the consequences.

4. The Hebrews, being of Abraham's descent, would have looked very different from the Canaanites. Anyone could have spotted Rahab with a Hebrew and reported it.

5. She had every reason *not* to help them; stopping them in their mission might have saved her people and her city.

Yet, Rahab did reach out to the men who came to spy out Jericho. Why?

A primary reason comes out of the text: she believed the God of the Hebrews was the true God (Joshua 2:9-13). She knew that the Lord had given them the land, and that no one could stand up to the Hebrews. She'd heard how God "dried up the water of the Red Sea" for them and how the kings of the Amorites had been destroyed. As a result, she said their hearts (the Canaanites) "melted" and no man had any courage. It was total despair—like a Little League team that learns its next game is against the New York Yankees, or finding out that Mr. T is coming to your house to fight you.

Rahab saw that the Hebrews were her only chance for survival. She was convinced God would not only defeat Jericho, but would leave nothing standing.

But beyond that, she had faith. The New Testament tells us, "By faith the prostitute, Rahab, because she welcomed the spies, was not killed with those who were disobedient" (Hebrews 11:31). (The record later shows that Rahab married a man named Salmon who was an ancestor of Boaz, King David, and ultimately, Jesus Christ.)

Why is *faith* such a critical ingredient in the outlook

of people who help? Because faith produces love for God, love for His creation and people, and a desire to obey. This doesn't mean that people who don't have "born again" faith would never help anyone else. But I'm convinced that only *real* faith can produce *real* help, the kind that gives and keeps on giving, even if nothing is given in return.

WHY HELP THE NEEDY?

Why should Christians help people in need? Let me offer you several strong biblical reasons.

First, *God commands it.*

The first laws—the Ten Commandments—that God gave Israel pointed this out. "Do not kill; do not commit adultery; do not steal; do not bear false witness; do not covet." Aren't these principles simply ways to love your neighbor?

In the New Testament, we find such other commands as, "Offer hospitality to one another without grumbling" (1 Peter 4:9). "Be devoted to one another in brotherly love. Honor one another above yourselves . . . share with God's people who are in need. Practice hospitality" (Romans 12:10, 13). And 1 John 3:17: "If anyone has material possessions, and sees his brother in need but has no pity on him, how can the love of God be in him?"

Second, *helping the needy is right.*

Too many Christians have to wait for a "feeling," or the revelation of a special verse, or a sign from heaven that doing something is God's will. But when it comes to helping others we should need only one reason: it's right.

We don't need convincing reasons. We don't even need a pastor to give us the chapter and verse. We know that helping others is right because we know how we feel when others *don't* help us.

Third, *God promises to reward us for helping others.*

Ever catch yourself asking, "What's in it for me?" when someone asks you to help? The answer is "Plenty." God will reward all of us who have given in any way to others. In the Sermon on the Mount, Jesus said about giving to beggars, "Do not let your left hand know what your right hand is doing, so that your giving may be in secret. Then your Father, who sees what is done in secret, will reward you" (Matthew 6:3-4). Even if no one else sees, God sees. He knows what you've done and whom you've helped. None of it will be forgotten.

Fourth, *we love God.*

Need a good reason to offer help? Then do it because you love God. Even if you can't say that you love the person, do it for Him.

Very few, if any of us, can do much "out of the goodness" of our hearts, because there isn't much goodness in them. It's only because the Lord touches and fills us that we can truly give. Then our hearts *do* become good because they're filled with Him who is good.

Do you get the picture? You won't be ready to help others unless certain things are active in your life: faith, love for God, and obedience. The only way you'll beat your inhumanity to man is by letting the Son of man transform your humanity.

I often think of the story of "Little Annie" as told by Zig Ziglar in his book *See You at the Top.* Little Annie was labeled "a hopeless case" and was placed in a mental institution outside Boston. Her doctors classified her as hopelessly insane and confined her to a cage in the cellar of the hospital. Sometimes she would angrily attack anyone who came into her cage, and other times she would ignore them. She seemed a perfect example of a schizophrenic.

Nonetheless, an elderly nurse didn't give up on Annie. She began visiting her in her cage and even began leaving brownies and other goodies outside the door. Gradually, the doctors saw a change taking place. They moved Annie out of the cage and upstairs. Later, she was so much better, she was told she could leave the institution and go home. She was cured. But Little Annie didn't want to go. She decided to stay on and help other patients.

Years later, Queen Victoria pinned England's highest award on Helen Keller. She asked the famed blind and deaf woman what accounted for her tremendous achievements in life despite her handicaps. Helen Keller replied that all of it was because of one woman, Anne Sullivan—"Little Annie"—who had taught her to find the light in a world of darkness.

What about you? You may not be an Anne Sullivan. And you probably don't have a Helen Keller on your hands either. But remember: God will not give you any more than He knows you can take care of at the moment.

The question is: Will you take care of it?

8

JOSHUA AND CALEB

WHEN YOU HAVE TO STAND ALONE

The twelve men peered out over the rocks where they hid. The town was less than a hundred yards away.

Caleb turned to the man next to him, Palti. "This is the place for me. When we take the land, I'll request this spot from Moses."

Palti snorted. "Take the land? Not now."

Caleb stared at him. "What do you mean, 'Not now'?"

"Just what I said. You saw the men going in and out of there. They're all over six feet tall. Some must be seven or eight feet. They'll squash us like grasshoppers. We'll never take the land."

Caleb looked around at the men. Several hung their heads. Others looked angry. He said to Ammiel, "What about you? Do you think we can take it?"

Ammiel glanced at Palti, then shook his head. "Palti's right. This land *is* good, and there's plenty to eat; but it's not for us. We have women and children in our camp. These men, the sons of Anak, are fighters."

Joshua stepped forward. "Stop being fools. Have you forgotten Jehovah?"

"That's just who I'm remembering," said Palti. "Getting us through the Red Sea and all those plagues was fine. But when it comes to fighting, swords in hand, that's different. How can God help thousands of people fighting at the same time? It's impossible. We'll lose."

Caleb breathed deeply. "Are you saying that we're going to tell Moses we can't take the land and to go somewhere else?"

"Definitely," said Palti.

Caleb threw his staff to the ground. "Not me! Never. We can take it! What are you—cowards?"

He gazed fiercely at each man. Only Joshua didn't hang his head. He walked over and stood next to Caleb. He whispered, "Let's not push it too hard, Caleb. We just need to see a little more."

Caleb responded angrily, "They've been talking like this ever since we saw these so-called sons of Anak. Now they're comparing us to grasshoppers."

"Calm down," said Joshua gently. "Let's get on with the mission."

Caleb glanced around, then picked up his staff. "I, for one, will hear no more about this." The men shifted their positions, then began filing out toward the valleys.

On the last night of their journey, the men sat around a campfire. Caleb brought up the issue again. "What do we tell Moses tomorrow?"

Palti said nothing, though Caleb looked at him first. No one spoke.

Finally Caleb said, "Palti—what about you?"

"I'm holding my own counsel. No more arguments."

Caleb set his jaw. "I'm saying we go in."

"Say what you want," said Palti. "There are eleven

others. We each have an opinion."

"Then what are your opinions?"

Joshua spoke up. "We go in. There can be no question."

The others were silent.

Caleb stood and kicked at the grass. "I want that land, men. I want it. You can't stop this. Anyone who speaks against taking the land will have me to reckon with."

Joshua stood up and walked over to Caleb, putting his arm on his shoulder. "Jehovah is in charge here, Caleb. Let's not provoke a fight where there is no fight."

Caleb shook Joshua's arm off. "They're going to ruin it. I know it. They're all cowards. COWARDS!" He looked around at the men.

Joshua took him aside, away from the fire. "Jehovah will triumph in these matters, Caleb. Leave it in His hands."

Caleb breathed deeply, looking into Joshua's eyes. "We'll see."

The twelve spies gave their report the next day. As Caleb had predicted, the other ten voiced great doubt. Moments later, the crowd was in an uproar. People shouted vengefully.

"God brought us out here to kill us."

"This is worse than Egypt!"

"It's been lies all along, nothing but lies."

"Our women and children will all die."

Suddenly, Caleb stood up before the people, holding up his hands. There was quiet.

"There's nothing to fear. By all means, we should go up and take the land—now. There's no question, we'll overcome. No one has stood before us. No one will."

Palti jumped up next to him. "It's suicide! We've seen the land. Ten of us say we can't take it. Aren't ten heads wiser than two? We can't go up against these people now. They're too strong for us."

Ammiel jumped up and said, "Every man we saw was huge—over eight feet tall."

Palti added, "I felt like a grasshopper before them. And I could tell, they thought of us as grasshoppers."

People shrieked and cried out. All night they wept in their tents. In the morning, a throng of men gathered, demanding that Moses be thrown out. "We want a new leader," Palti said.

Moses and Aaron came out of their tents and fell on their faces. Caleb was enraged. Both he and Joshua tore their cloaks in anguish.

"The land we've seen is a good land," shouted Caleb. "If God is pleased with us, He'll bring us into it and give it to us. Don't rebel now. Don't fear these people—they're nothing. God has removed their protection and is with *us.*"

But people picked up stones and glared at him. Joshua turned to Caleb. "They're going to stone us."

Suddenly, God's pillar of fire roared above the meeting tent. The crowd fell back. God spoke to Moses in a voice of thunder. "How long will these people spurn Me? And how long will they not believe in Me?"

As you probably know, the people didn't go into the land then. In fact, they had to wait another forty years, until every man over twenty years old (except Joshua and Caleb) had died. The ten cowardly spies suffered immediately, though. A plague struck all of them and they died.

It's not an uncommon situation. Christians frequently find themselves standing alone in the midst of a crowd of unbelievers. Their convictions and beliefs are often laughed at and ridiculed.

I remember hearing a story about a college student who had a class in which the professor repeatedly ridiculed the Bible. One day the prof launched into a particularly nasty tirade. Suddenly, he looked out over the class. "None of you believe that book, do you? None of you are that stupid, I hope."

The student raised his hand.

The prof eyed him. "You believe the Bible?"

"Yes."

The prof snorted and looked around, cracked a few jokes, and made the student look like a fool. Then he said, "I've read the Bible from beginning to end and none of it ever made any sense to me."

The student decided to speak. "Sir, the Bible is a love letter from God to His beloved children. If you don't understand what it says, then that's what you get for reading other people's mail."

The class erupted with laughter. One small step for Christians; one giant step for Christiankind!

TEN WERE BAD AND TWO WERE GOOD

Going back to the story of the twelve spies, can you imagine the tension and anger both Caleb and Joshua felt for the other ten? Here, for the last few years, they'd all seen God's miracles multiplied. They watched as God made a mockery of the gods of Egypt. Every one of the ten plagues destroyed the supposed power of some Egyptian god. If there was ever any question about which god had the power and the glory, there should no longer have been any after the plagues.

But Israel refused to believe. When God let them leave Egypt, Pharaoh gathered his chariot army and thundered out after Moses and the children of Israel. God helped them miraculously escape the Egyptians by dividing the Red Sea. Israel walked through the walls of water like they were taking a Sabbath stroll. The moment they reached the other side, and the Egyptian chariots started into the sea after them, God closed back the walls of water and drowned the Egyptian charioteers in the sea.

But somehow it wasn't enough for the Israelites. God followed these miracles up with others—turning bitter water into fresh water (Exodus 15:22-26), providing manna every morning for months (Exodus 16), bringing water out of a rock (Exodus 17:1-7), defeating the Amalekites (Exodus 17:8-13), and appearing to all Israel on Mt. Sinai and thundering the Ten Commandments to them in His own voice (Exodus 19–20). Even more miracles followed. But were they enough to convince Israel that God was God and no one could successfully oppose Him? No. The Israelites were hard in heart, rebellious and unbelieving. And no amount of miracles will sway an unbeliever if he chooses not to believe.

Isn't that remarkable? I used to think that in witnessing, if you could come up with enough evidence, people would be compelled to believe. Not so. Miracles will *help* a person toward belief, if the Spirit is working in him. But if a person is hardened in his unbelief, not even a display of God's power will look convincing. Consider the Pharisees. They saw Jesus perform hundreds, if not thousands, of miracles—healings of blind and deaf men, people who were lame for years, men who suffered from demon possession, even the raising of dead people. Yet, what was their conclusion? "He [Jesus] has a demon!"

How could they think that? Easy. If a man chooses to reject Christ, and the Spirit has chosen no longer to draw him, nothing will turn that man back.

It can be the most frustrating experience on earth.

And I'm certain that's precisely what Joshua and Caleb felt. Here they'd seen miracle after miracle, display of power after display of power, and yet the other ten were saying that the land couldn't be taken. How blind could they be?

PRINCIPLES FOR STANDING ALONE

Yet, out of this passage arises several important principles about standing alone. By understanding these truths, we become better equipped to endure when everyone else around us stumbles.

First, *remember that God's jobs are always bigger than you are.*

The problem for the ten spies was the monstrous size of the task at hand. All the spies could think of was what their motley band looked like—women, children, donkeys, sheep, and oxen. All the men of Israel had been slaves, and purposely unlearned in the ways of war. The job simply looked like too much for the sedate band of Israel.

But that is always God's way. He always gives His people something far greater than they could ever think of attempting on their own. Why? To make it clear later that *He* accomplished the victory!

Do you remember the story of Gideon? The Midianites had raided Israel so often that hardly a grain of wheat was left. So God raised up Gideon to form an army and drive the Midianites out. Gideon called all able men to join him. And how many showed up? 32,000! It was a miracle. But then God stepped in and said there were too many, that Gideon had to cut it down. So Gideon told everyone who was afraid to go home. Twenty-two thousand left! But that left 10,000 men, and that's still quite an army (though the Midianites had over 120,000 men).

But God was still displeased. Gideon had to sift out

some more. In the end, he was left with 300 men to battle 120,000.

Why did God do this? He told Gideon it was because he had "too many men for Me to deliver Midian into their hands." He didn't want Israel to "boast against Me that her own strength has saved her" (Judges 7:2).

God wants people to know He is great and good, and nothing is too difficult for Him. Why? So that His people will fix their trust in Him even more firmly.

Second, *remember that anytime you proceed on an action that requires faith, you will be opposed.*

Why were the other ten spies afraid? They'd seen God's miracles. They had God's promises.

Why were they afraid then? Because they had no faith. "For God did not give us a spirit of timidity but a spirit of power, of love, and of self-discipline" (2 Timothy 1:7). "There is no fear in love. But perfect love drives out fear, because fear has to do with punishment. The man who fears is not made perfect in love" (1 John 4:18). If you confront an impossible job that appears to be far bigger than anything you can overcome, and you do not have faith in the God who is bigger than all, you will be afraid.

That's exactly what happened to the spies. It's a process:

Doubt leads to
discouragement, which leads to
distrust, which leads to
disobedience, which leads to
disowning God, which results in
destruction.

The spies had no faith; they doubted God. They saw the sons of Anak and became discouraged. Their discouragement led them to distrust God, saying He either brought them into the wilderness by mistake or to kill them. Distrust resulted in disobedience: they refused to go in and conquer. Disobedience eventually resulted in disowning, or abandoning any trust in God. In fact, they may even have gone to the other extreme, calling Him a fraud, or a cheat, or worse, saying He didn't exist at all. That disowning finally ended in destruction.

"But what about Joshua and Caleb?" you may be asking. "They had faith."

That's just the point. Anyone with faith will be opposed by those who don't have it. To the faithless, anything God wants us to do looks absurd. "It can't be done," they say. Anytime you act in faith, you will discover multitudes of people who will seek to throw you off balance, or who will attempt to make you compromise your convictions.

Third, *remember that sometimes, while you are acting in faith, God will allow you to be overcome even though you're doing right.*

I'm certain that the hardest moment for Joshua and Caleb was when God issued the decree that Israel would not go into the land (Numbers 14:20-25). "But why?" Caleb might have shouted. "*I* believe! Why should their unbelief ruin Your plan?"

Sometimes God allows the faithful to be overcome, overthrown, even killed by the unfaithful. That's certainly the hardest aspect of standing alone. Here, you've given your all. You've stayed with the faith. You've supported God. But you too go down with the ship!

We must remember that God's way is not our way. He has an overall purpose and plan that will ultimately give Him the glory and us the greatest joy we could imagine. Sometimes a part of that plan looks utterly ridiculous. We can't understand how God could let something bad happen to men of faith.

Being right does not mean being victorious. Being faithful does not mean being successful. Remember that when you stand alone. You're where you are because God put you there. He has a plan and a purpose for you to be there. But if you can't see it, that doesn't make it any less glorious.

So it was with Joshua and Caleb. When God allowed the unbelievers to triumph and suddenly the two faithful spies realized they would have forty years of wandering and pain ahead of them, they must have been tempted to cry out, "It's not fair!" But they didn't. They were men of faith who believed in the God who was wise, kind, and knew exactly what He was doing from the very beginning.

But they could easily have become bitter, or even tried to take matters into their own hands. That leads us to a fourth principle:

Fourth, *let God deal with the opposition.*

When you stand alone and are opposed, the people on the opposite side will often hurl harsh words at you. Even a believer can be tempted to take revenge, to see those people get what they deserve.

But in this instance, once the decision was made, Joshua and Caleb were silent. They didn't whip out their swords and begin hacking at the other ten; nor did they shout curses and taunts at them. They waited on God. And God acted. He sent a plague that immediately killed all ten of the opposition.

Waiting on God is difficult. But He promises that He will repay. When Paul was opposed by Alexander, he didn't resort to threats. He simply told Timothy, "The Lord will repay him for what he has done" (2 Timothy 4:14). We can be sure that when we stand alone, *God* will deal with our enemies.

Finally, when you stand alone, *remember that your job is to obey the Lord regardless of what others do;*

ultimately, He will vindicate you.

It may take years. It took forty years for Caleb and Joshua. But in the end, they survived, went into the land, and were ultimately remembered as great saints of God. But those other ten? Can you even name one of them? They're gone, buried, and forgotten until that last day when they arise and stand before God to answer for their sins.

When we stand alone, many temptations come at us. The desire for revenge, for vindication, for the world to see that we're right. Don't give in to those temptations. God will vindicate you, and one day you will "appear with Him in glory" (Colossians 3:4).

I think of the story of Eric Liddell in *Chariots of Fire* and how he wouldn't run in a track meet on a Sunday. Everyone laughed. Then came that day when he ran the four hundred meters in the Olympics. He not only won the gold, but his exuberant style and faithful witness won many hearts. He became the hero of multitudes. The movie ends with a statement about his death in a prison camp in China at the end of World War II: "All of Scotland mourned."

That's what the world thinks of someone who stands for what is right, who stands on his convictions, who stands in faith. That's what the world thinks of him who stands alone, though at the time of his standing, they may have been spitting in his face.

9

PAUL AND SILAS

REJOICING IN THE MIDST OF TROUBLE

For six days in a row, the demon-possessed girl had
followed the men. Today was no different. She was
shrieking in that same guttural, demonic voice, "These
men are servants of the Most High God who are telling you the way to be saved."

People along the roadway snickered at the two men
to whom she referred. Paul and Silas walked along,
tired and upset.

"How long do we have to put up with this?" asked
Silas.

Paul breathed heavily. Suddenly, he set his lips and
turned.

The demon-possessed girl stopped and stared wildly
at him. Her eyes seemed almost not to see. Her face
was twisted and she looked tired, as though she were
weary of doing something, but unable to stop.

Paul looked into her eyes. "In the name of Jesus
Christ, I command you—"

There was a dramatic pause. The people along the
roadway stopped and stared. The girl flinched, stum-
bling backwards.

"Come out of her!" Paul said fiercely.

The girl's face contorted. She grabbed her throat. She gagged, her eyes widened, and she let out a scream. Then she fell forward.

Paul and Silas rushed to her side. They fell to their knees and cradled her head.

She looked into their eyes. "I . . . I don't understand," she said.

Paul smiled. "You have been released."

She gazed at him. "I feel so . . . new," she said slowly. "What happened?"

"The demons who possessed you have been cast out," said Silas. "You were released by the power of the Lord Jesus."

The girl looked from Silas to Paul. "What am I to do?"

"Believe on Jesus and repent of your sins," Paul said gently. "Follow the Lord Jesus and be His disciple. There are some others who meet down by the water. We'll introduce them to you."

At that moment, an angry man rushed up and pushed Paul and Silas back. "What's going on here? Chandra, what has happened?" He stared at the girl.

"These men, they—"

Paul stepped up. "Christ, through us, has cast out the demon that possessed her. She is free."

The man's face twisted into a snarl. "You cast out the demon!" He turned to some men who were with him. "Grab them. Bring them to the magistrates."

Chandra sat on the ground. The man looked at her. "I'll deal with you later, slave. And it won't be pretty."

She shrank back.

Two men grabbed Paul and two others grabbed Silas. They dragged them through Philippi to the magistrate's office.

When they got there, the man, whose name was

Marius, pounded his fist on the magistrate's table and began to shout. A crowd was forming.

"These men are throwing our city into confusion. They're Jews, and they're proclaiming customs and religions which are not lawful for Romans to accept. They must be dealt with immediately."

The magistrate spoke with a nasal tone, "Beat them with rods."

"This'll teach you to cast demons out of our slaves," seethed Marius.

Two officers came in holding birch rods. "How many strokes?" asked one.

Marius glanced at the magistrate and said, "Until I say stop."

Paul and Silas were thrust to the ground. The officers stood over them and began the beatings. After ten minutes, Paul fainted. Silas lasted two more minutes and then he fainted. When they awoke, they found themselves being dragged to a prison.

"Is this lawful?" rasped Silas to Paul.

"No," Paul said.

When they reached the prison, the jailer immediately took them down three stone stairways to the dungeon. He locked their hands and feet in stocks. Their backs were bleeding.

"I can hardly breathe," wheezed Silas when the jailer was gone.

"Rest," said Paul, "and find a comfortable position."

Both men closed their eyes. Paul prayed, "Lord, give us sleep. Give us relief from pain." Moments later they were asleep.

Shortly after nightfall, Silas awoke. "Paul," he whispered, "Paul!"

Paul awoke with a start and looked around. The pain in his back was unbearable.

"What are we going to do?" Silas whispered.

Paul wrestled with the stocks, trying to find a comfortable position. "Pray," he said suddenly.

Silas wrenched his neck and looked at him. A slow smile came to his lips. "You go first."

Paul began praying through David's Psalms, adding his own comments. For an hour they alternated both Psalms and supplications to the Lord, praying for the people of Philippi: Chandra, Lydia, even Marius and the jailer.

When they finished, Paul said, "Now we sing."

Silas smiled. "Which song?"

Paul named a tune. The two men sang psalms and hymns of praise to God. Twice they stopped. But when they did, several prisoners shouted, "Sing more. We like what you're singing." So they continued singing for the men.

As they sang, there was a sudden shudder. The ground underneath them quaked. The stone walls rattled. The mortar between the stones came loose. The spikes holding the stocks in place creaked and loosened. In a moment, Paul and Silas were free. They stood up.

"God is releasing us," said Silas.

Paul shook his head. "No. It's something else. Wait."

The whole prison shook. Then there was silence. Men called out to one another.

Paul shouted, "Everyone stay where you are." His voice was insistent, so the men listened.

A moment later, the jailer ran in with a sword and torch and looked around. Paul and Silas watched him.

The jailer panicked. "Everyone's escaped," he shouted.

Immediately, Paul called to him, "We're all here."

The man peered at him through the darkness and advanced. "Are there others?" he asked, astounded.

"All of us," said Paul.

"We've heard about the Christ!" came a shout over the walls.

"We believe," said another.

The man looked at Paul. "They all stayed because of you?"   *jailer*

Paul shook his head. "No. Because of the Lord Jesus. I didn't realize the men had believed. But . . . "

The jailer released Paul and Silas and took them upstairs.

Suddenly, he fell at Paul's feet. "Sirs, what must I do to be saved?"

Paul began to explain the Gospel. He concluded, "Believe on the Lord Jesus and you will be saved, you and your household."

jailer The man bowed his head. "I believe. Come to my house, please. I will give you dinner and bathe your wounds. You can tell my family this story."

Paul looked at Silas and shook his head. "God's wonders never end!" he said.

narator

Read the rest of the account in Acts 16. It is truly an amazing story. Here were two men, beaten and bloody, praying and singing to God while they were in prison. We could believe it if they were cursing, or pleading for release, or calling for lightning bolts to come down on their persecutors. But hymns and prayers?

Rejoicing in the midst of trial is a distinctive mark of the Christian. No other faith on earth has such an outlook. Christians are instructed to rejoice in every imaginable circumstance.

Jesus said, "I have told you these things, so that in Me you may have peace. In this world you will have trouble. But take heart! I have overcome the world" (John 16:33).

He said in the Sermon on the Mount, "Blessed are you when people insult you, persecute you and falsely say all kinds of evil against you because of Me. Rejoice and be glad, because great is your reward in heaven" (Matthew 5:11-12).

Paul said, "We also rejoice in our sufferings because we know that suffering produces perseverance; perseverance, character; and character, hope. And hope does not disappoint us, because God has poured out His love into our hearts by the Holy Spirit whom He has given us" (Romans 5:3-5).

He advised the Philippians, the very people who witnessed him and Silas rejoicing in prison, "Rejoice in the Lord always. I will say it again: Rejoice!" (Philippians 4:4) In fact, the Philippian letter is one constant reminder to rejoice during trying circumstances.

James said it this way: "Consider it pure joy, my brothers, whenever you face trials of many kinds, because you know that the testing of your faith develops perseverance" (James 1:2-3).

And Peter said, "Dear friends, do not be surprised at the painful trial you are suffering, as though something strange were happening to you. But rejoice that you participate in the sufferings of Christ" (1 Peter 4:12-13).

What does the world say? "Complain." "Get even." "Fight fire with fire."

But God says, "Rejoice." How is this possible?

THE ONLY WAY TO GET THE REJOICING OUTLOOK

The only way to get the rejoicing outlook is to have a correct understanding of certain elements of God's nature.

1. *You must believe God is sovereign.*

"I am the Lord, and there is no other; apart from Me there is no God" (Isaiah 45:5).

"For He spoke, and it came to be; He commanded, and it stood firm. The Lord foils the plans of the nations; He thwarts the purposes of the peoples. But the plans of the Lord stand firm forever, the purposes of His heart through all generations" (Psalm 33:9-11).

He "works out everything in conformity with the purpose of His will" (Ephesians 1:11).

God rules. He's in charge. No one can subvert Him, overrule Him, defeat Him, or catch Him off guard. He planned both the beginning and the end before anything existed.

God *is* sovereign. He "calls the shots." That doesn't mean He *causes* everything that happens, including sin and evil. No, He never causes evil, or even uses it. But so long as evil exists (one day He will end it entirely), He has chosen to let it do certain things. But His allowance in that area does not make Him the cause of evil.

Furthermore, He allows evil to exist only within certain limits. He actively prevents it from going too far. At times He chooses to stop it altogether. But for the most part, He, as ruler and king, has chosen to allow evil to take its course, all the while working around it to aid, strengthen, and build His own people.

That's the reason Paul and Silas could rejoice in their miserable situation. They knew God was in charge. For some reason He had allowed it, and, therefore, they could be content in that. They knew if He had chosen not to allow things to happen, those things wouldn't have happened. But since He, in His role as perfect Lord and Master, had chosen to allow them to be subjected to tough circumstances, they would submit to Him and follow.

That doesn't mean that anytime anything bad happens we should lie down and play dead. In fact, in this very passage, Paul asserted his rights as a Roman citizen. In Acts 16:36-37 the jailer came to Paul and told him to leave quietly. But Paul said, "They beat us publicly without a trial, even though we are Roman citizens, and threw us into prison. And now do they want to get rid of us quietly? No! Let them come themselves and escort us out."

It was unlawful for a Roman citizen to be beaten or judged without a trial before Roman magistrates. In this case, those rules weren't followed. As a Roman, Paul had a right to demand certain privileges. Thus, he didn't simply fall down like a carpet and let them walk all over him, saying, "God is sovereign; therefore, I should just take it." No, where God has provided legal protection, we have every right to use it. Rejoicing in tribulation because God is sovereign does not mean being totally passive to every situation. Rather, it means active confrontation—first, through submitting to God's lordship by rejoicing and acknowledging Him; and second, through exercising whatever legal pathways we have to get rid of the circumstance. Rejoicing in God's sovereignty never means laying down your rightful arms and playing dead.

2. *You must believe God is purposeful in His actions.*

Believing that God is sovereign is one thing; but you must also recognize that God has reasons for what He's doing. That is, He's not some unpredictable ruler who does something just because He happens to feel like it at the moment. Rather, everything that happens in life happens because God has allowed it for ultimate good.

This doesn't mean that God lets some evil happen to someone because He knows it will lead to good. No, it means that while someone has chosen to do something bad, God can still work around it and ultimately cause a good result.

Understand, I'm not mixing up words here. There is

a difference between manipulating evil (which God never does) and letting evil happen which He intends to work around. In the first case, manipulating evil is evil in itself. But working around evil that happens leaves Him clean and untouched. He didn't cause the evil. He didn't hope it would occur. He didn't do anything to make it happen. Evil generated itself. And God chose to limit it and work around it so that good resulted.

That's one reason Silas and Paul rejoiced. They knew not only that their beating and imprisonment was under God's control, but that God had allowed it for a reason—a good reason. Even if they didn't know the reason, they could trust God because they knew He Himself was good, kind, compassionate, holy, and righteous and that He would never do anything to destroy them.

3. *You must believe God is wise.*

"OK, God is sovereign, and all that He does has a purpose. But is His purpose the best purpose?" In other words, "Does God know what He's doing?"

If Paul and Silas were in prison because God allowed it for a purpose, that's nice. But Paul could say, "I disagree with You, Lord. I don't think you should have allowed this. There's a better way." This is why it's critical that a rejoicer believe that God is wise.

"Do not deceive yourselves. If any one of you thinks he is wise by the standards of this age, he should become a 'fool' so that he may become wise. For the wisdom of this world is foolishness in God's sight. As it is written: 'He catches the wise in their craftiness'; and again, " 'The Lord knows that the thoughts of the wise are futile' " (1 Corinthians 3:18-20).

God's wisdom means that He uses His knowledge—His omniscience—to execute that plan which is most perfectly in line with His purposes. That is, He has chosen to allow certain things to happen according to His wisdom. He's leading it all to a perfect, wise, just, and good result.

In my life I've often argued with God about one incident. My daughter was born six weeks early, weighed four pounds, and had to be hooked up to a heart and breathing monitor to live. My first impulse was to ask, "Why, God? What's the point? Why did this have to happen?"

God rarely answers such questions. In fact, to this day I don't see any particular wisdom about that situation. But I do know God is wise. I do know that He knows why He did it and that what He did was perfect. "I know that everything God does will endure forever; nothing can be added to it and nothing can be taken from it. God does it so men will revere Him" (Ecclesiastes 3:14). "He is the Rock, His words are perfect" (Deuteronomy 32:4). Therefore, I can rejoice and trust Him, even though I may not understand.

Years ago, my parents had a little dog named Jed. He looked a lot like a cocker spaniel, but he was a mutt. He and I had a fairly good relationship. He seemed to trust me more than other dogs we had. Jed hated one thing: going to the vet. One afternoon I helped my mother take him in because she was afraid he'd fight her all the way. She was right. But somehow we got him into the checkup room. I breathed a sigh of relief and went out to read a magazine.

Moments later there was a yelp. The door opened and Jed rushed out into my arms. He looked into my eyes as if to say, "You won't let him touch me, will you?"

I tried to reassure him, then took him back in. He needed a shot, so I held him gently and spoke to him as he lay on the slab. He didn't move. His eyes remained fixed on mine, as if to say, "OK, if you say it's all right, I'll hang tough." He received his shot without a whimper.

Simple as that is, it's like God's wisdom. How could I explain to Jed about shots, bacteria, antibodies, and so on? It would be impossible. Much less can God explain why bad things happen to us in life. But He can speak reassuring words to us. He can say, "Trust Me. I know what I'm doing. Everything's under control, even though it may not look that way to you." As Solomon said, "Lean not on your own understanding" (Proverbs 3:5). That is, stop trying to figure it out for yourself and leave it in God's hands. He knows what He's doing.

4. *You must believe God loves you.*

God's sovereignty can seem distant and uncaring. His purposefulness says *His* purpose is in effect, but what about *my* good and *my* needs? His wisdom tells us He knows what He's doing, but does that wisdom apply to me?

That's where love comes in. God's love for each one of us is boundless and infinite.

"God is love" (1 John 4:16).

"God so loved the world that He gave His one and only Son" (John 3:16).

"He who did not spare His own Son, but gave Him up for us all—how will He not also, along with Him, graciously give us all things?" (Romans 8:32)

God's love holds it all together. Knowing He loves us gives us security. Knowing that everything that happens proceeds from a heart of love allows us to rejoice in even the worst circumstances.

WHAT HAPPENED?

But was that the end of the story? Not at all. Look at the great results of Paul and Silas' obedience:

1. The prisoners listened to Paul and Silas as they prayed and sang. Undoubtedly, some became believers and, eventually, members of the church in Philippi.

2. The jailer believed, with all his household.

3. The magistrates and everyone else saw the work of God—from the exorcism of the demon-possessed girl, to the earthquake at the prison, to the new church founded in Philippi.

4. A church was established to which Paul later wrote the Epistle to the Philippians.

God did bring good out of the evil situation.

Anne Steele (1716–1788) suffered many heartaches during her long life. At age three, her mother died. As a child, she was fragile. Tuberculosis threatened to consume her constantly. At age nineteen, she had an accident that injured her hip and left her nearly invalid. As a result, she spent long hours alone in her room. Nonetheless, she met a young man, Robert Elscourt, and when she was twenty-one, they decided to marry. Preparations were made. She looked excitedly toward her wedding day. But tragedy struck once again. Robert drowned the evening before the wedding.

One could easily understand any bitterness Anne might have felt toward God. But she chose instead to rejoice, even in heartache. She poured out her grief by writing songs and hymns of praise to God. One of them, written some time after Robert's tragic death, contained these words:

Father, whate'er of earthly bliss Thy sov'reign will denies,

Accepted at Thy throne of grace, Let this petition rise:

Give me a calm, a thankful heart, From every murmur free;

The blessings of Thy grace impart, And let me live to Thee.

(*Living Stories of Famous Hymns,* Ernest K. Emurian, Baker, 1955; pp. 40–42).

Nothing could produce an outlook like that in Anne Steele, except the Spirit of God. That same Spirit works in you, if you are a Christian. Ask Him to guide you to all the truth about God—not just His sovereignty, purpose, wisdom, and love, but all there is to know about Him. As you grow in that knowledge, your heart will learn to rejoice in all circumstances of life.

10

KING SAUL

HANDLING JEALOUSY BEFORE IT HANDLES YOU

The moment the stone struck, Goliath fell. David rushed forward and cut off his head, then held it up for all the soldiers to see. Immediately, the Israelite army jumped forward to engage the remaining Philistines.

After the battle, all the men spoke of the courage and finesse of David. King Saul himself met David at the top of the hill. "Whose son are you, young man?"

David replied, "I am the son of your servant, Jesse of Bethlehem."

Saul smiled. "You'll be in my house from now on. I want you not only as my psalmist, but also to command a hundred men."

David felt his heart jolt. He'd dreamed of this moment. "Yes, sir."

Later, Saul's son Jonathan took David aside to talk to him. In a few hours, they were fast friends.

The army was in the field for two more weeks. Finally it came time to return to the king's home in Gibeah. King Saul loved going through the cities with the army of Israel. With each town came a new greeting, new applause, and new compliments. He never tired of it.

As they approached the city of Elam, all the young women ran out with tambourines. One walked up to the king.

"We have a song for you, our lord, and for David, the slayer of Goliath."

Saul smiled. "Play," he said, and kicked his horse to move forward.

The women began to sing. It was a happy song, full of the details of Israel's conquests and Saul's victories over Edom, Moah, Zobah, and the Amalekites. Then the chorus:

"Saul has slain his thousands,
And David his ten thousands."

At first, Saul wasn't sure what had been said. But he listened intently. "Thousands . . . ten thousands," he muttered. His face clouded over and he glanced at Jonathan. But his son didn't seem to understand what was being said. Jonathan simply smiled at the women and laughed.

A woman walked up to David, bowed, then gave him a rose. "For saving us all," she said.

Saul felt the anger burn in his belly. *Is my son such a fool he doesn't know what has been said?* he thought. *Already he's given that young boar David his robe. Listen, Jonathan,* he shouted in his mind, *they've ascribed ten thousands to David and only thousands to me! Now what more can he have but the kingdom?*

Saul gave his horse another kick. "Let's get through this town quickly. There will be bigger ones as we go along," he said.

They passed through more cities. In each one, all the women sang the same song. That night in Gibeah, Saul was enraged. But he decided to say nothing.

The best thing to do is wait, he thought. *He'll make a*

mistake. I'll put him in the hardest fighting position possible.

The next day Saul was depressed. David was called in to play the lyre.

Saul stalked through the house raving. His words made no sense. He held a spear in his hand. David watched him carefully, wondering what was wrong. Each time Saul walked into the room with the spear, David tensed. *He wouldn't throw it at me, would he?* David wondered. He tried to play joyously, but he found himself in fear of the king.

Suddenly, Saul hurled the spear. David saw him and jumped aside. The spear knocked over a pitcher of water and sliced into the wall. David ran out of the room.

Outside, he found Jonathan. "Your father—" he said breathlessly, "your father just hurled a spear at me. What's wrong with him?"

Jonathan sighed heavily and took David aside. "He's been like that for several years now. Ever since the Amalekites . . . " His voice trailed off.

"Well, what happened? What's wrong?"

"Samuel told him his kingdom would not stand. He said that God had torn it away from him."

David remembered when Samuel had come and anointed *him* king. In a way, he didn't quite believe it at the time. But Samuel was the revered prophet and judge of Israel. He had even anointed Saul. David had decided to wait and see what would happen.

Could Saul be jealous of me? he wondered. Suddenly he felt afraid.

Jonathan put his hand on David's shoulder. "Don't worry. God is with you. And we're friends. My father won't hurt you."

David wanted to believe him. As he walked back to

the house, he thought. *This is even worse than Goliath. That was easy. But what if your own king is against you?* Inside the house, he picked up his lyre and waited for Saul to return.

We call it the "green-eyed monster." But it's more than a monster. It's a murderer of men, an annihilator of the heart. Jealousy can destroy a person like nothing else.

It comes and goes. It's usually just a little "twinge," just a moment of wishing you had something someone else has. But sometimes it can take over your life. With King Saul, David became an obsession. Destroying David became the focus of his life.

THREE POWERFUL EFFECTS

Saul's jealousy was accompanied by other significant emotions: anger, suspicion, and fear. We find him angry in 1 Samuel 18:8 when the women sing their songs comparing Saul's and David's conquests. He was angry that they'd forgotten him so quickly. It didn't seem fair.

Saul's anger gave way to suspicion. "And Saul looked at David with suspicion from that day on" (1 Samuel 18:9, NASB). This usually happens to people in high positions who are jealous of others working their way up.

Suspicion led to a third emotion: fear. "Saul was afraid of David, because the Lord was with David but had left Saul" (1 Samuel 18:12). Saul recognized that David had what *he* had once had: God's Spirit and anointing. It made Saul afraid.

That's the point at which jealousy becomes a destructive monster. You end up being fearful of the very people who care about you. Jealousy can eat you up.

SAUL'S REACTIONS

Saul took several actions that are typical of most jealous people.

1. THE OVERREACTION

The first thing that happened was sheer lunacy. Saul began throwing his spear at David regularly. We find him doing this on at least three occasions, twice according to 1 Samuel 18:11 and again in 1 Samuel 19:10. A fourth time he threw his spear at his own son, Jonathan (1 Samuel 20:33).

Saul had lost all presence of mind—a common result of jealousy. Jealousy overpowers you, crushes you. You lash out. You do crazy things. You throw lamps, books, hatchets! You smash your fist into the wall. You scream and shout.

But you quickly find that for every action there is an equal and opposite reaction. The person you're jealous of may begin doing things in return. Or you may simply suffer the consequences of your own stupidity. (Smashing your fist into a wall often results in a broken hand.)

2. THE SUBTLE APPROACH

There's more than one way to skin a cat. Saul came up with another plan. He promoted David to commander of 1,000 men. He even offered David his daughter in marriage, saying, "I will give her to you in marriage; only serve me bravely and fight the battles of the Lord" (1 Samuel 18:17). Saul thought, "If you can't beat him, pretend to join him." He figured that putting David in the midst of all the hot battles would surely do him in.

The amazing thing is that David wouldn't accept the wife because he felt unworthy, but he kept right on fighting the Lord's battles—and winning. Saul came to dread him even more.

Then Saul came up with another ploy. A second

daughter, Michal, loved David and wanted to marry him. He offered David her hand openly, but David refused, still insisting that he was unworthy to be the king's son-in-law. Then Saul got really smart. He began to realize that David liked tests of strength and skill. So he had his servants tell David that he could have the girl if David killed 100 Philistines and brought the king their foreskins (a rather incredible idea). Saul thought David would surely die trying to perform this feat.

But David went out with his men and killed *200* Philistines and brought their foreskins to Saul. The result was that he got Michal, and Saul became "still more afraid of him, and he remained his enemy the rest of his days" (1 Samuel 18:29). Saul became hardened in his opposition. And since his subtle approach didn't work, Saul tried a different method.

3. GET OTHERS TO DO YOUR DIRTY WORK

Saul asked Jonathan and his attendants to kill David (1 Samuel 19:1). But they all loved him and warned him what Saul was doing. David escaped.

It's strange, but when you're jealous, you tend to lose perspective about everything else. How could Saul think that Jonathan and the others would listen to him and commit murder? His jealousy had become a raging obsession. He wasn't thinking realistically anymore. It had overtaken him.

4. LET JEALOUSY BECOME A CRAVEN OBSESSION

Eventually all of Saul's efforts failed. David only increased in stature. At that point, Saul reacted by banishing David from the kingdom, and beginning his own "search and destroy" mission. Saul became bent on eliminating David forever.

This kind of obsession is still prevalent today. Often I've seen men in viable ministries caught in the snare of jealousy. They're jealous of anyone who speaks well, writes well, ministers well, or is spoken of well by others. They can't even bear to hear the other person's name. It's foolish, but it's real. And it's potent.

HOW DO YOU DEAL WITH JEALOUSY?

What do you do if you're caught in this downward spiral? How do you get out of it?

The first thing to do is recognize it for what it is. When you feel all that anger and suspicion directed at someone, start asking yourself why. What is it that they have, or that you fear?

Notice that Saul never seemed to recognize his jealousy for what it was. All along he attributed the problem to the existence of David. If only David weren't around, all would be well. Saul's problem was his refusal to recognize sin. It's the worst sort of self-deception.

The Lord's command to all of us is, "Come now, let us reason together. . . . Though your sins are like scarlet, they shall be white as snow" (Isaiah 1:18). Recognize the sin. Stop deceiving yourself.

Second, admit your jealousy to the Lord. "If we confess our sins, He is faithful and just and will forgive us our sins and purify us from all unrighteousness" (1 John 1:9). Confession and admission is cleansing. There's a release there. The burden drops away.

You simply can't defeat sin by pretending it's not sin or pretending it's not there. The way to destroy it is to face it. David Augsburger told a story in his book *The Freedom of Forgiveness* about anger being like a tiger. A certain tamer had a tiger that he put into a cage. The tiger roared and growled so much the tamer couldn't sleep. Sometimes the tiger would knock down the cage and get loose. The tamer tried everything to stop the tiger. But he was extremely afraid of it and wouldn't look it in the eye. The tiger knew he had control.

But one day after a terrific battle, the tamer decided to try something new. He faced the tiger with a cold glint in his eyes. At first, it was a tremendous struggle. The tiger bared his teeth, raked the air with his claws, and stared back at the tamer fiercely. But as the tamer kept staring, the tiger finally whimpered, lay down at his feet, and went to sleep.

In the same way, jealousy is something you have to face. Look at it. Stare it down. Admit it's there. Then take it to the Lord. Tell Him about it. He'll show you how to tame it.

Third, think about confessing it to others if the problem persists. James said, "Confess your sins to each other and pray for each other so that you may be healed" (James 5:16).

Confession of sin to God always obtains forgiveness. But sometimes it's necessary to enlist the aid of others through confession to experience true freedom. Their prayers, support, love, and understanding can help greatly.

This is precisely what Saul didn't do. He didn't discuss his sin with anyone. He didn't ask for anyone's help. He denied it to himself too. He told himself he didn't need help. He was the king. All he needed to do was get rid of David. As a result, Saul never found freedom. He died an unhappy, sinful man.

Fourth, renew your mind. Drink deeply of Scripture and what it says about you as a person so that jealousy is not something you feel. Paul tells us in Ephesians 4:22-24, "You were taught, with regard to your former way of life, to put off your old self, which is being corrupted by its deceitful desires; to be made new in the attitude of your minds; and to put on the new self, created to be like God in true righteousness and holiness."

Look at that process: PUT OFF; BE MADE NEW; PUT ON. That's a microcosm of the whole Christian life. Put off the old ways. Ask God to take them out of your life. Be renewed. Let your mind and heart be directed by what Scripture says. Put on the new person. Don those character traits and fruits of the Spirit: love, joy, peace, patience, kindness, goodness, faithfulness; gentleness, and self-control. Let them become the standards of your life.

You renew your mind by drenching it in Scripture. Memorize the Word. Get it into your heart. Then do as it says. Eventually, you'll see fruit popping out everywhere.

But Saul didn't do that either. Years later he'd completely forgotten about God, his Word, and His power. He went to a medium, the witch of Endor, and learned the last grim fact of his life. He and his son would die in the next battle.

Saul was a man possessed—possessed and driven by an inner obsession that tore his mind and heart to pieces. When it was all over, Saul was nothing but a jealous, old fool. His jealousy had destroyed him.

JEALOUSY DIVIDES

Jealousy divides man from man, brother from brother, husband from wife. It kills because it makes you angry, suspicious, afraid, and full of irrational and obsessive thoughts. Eventually, if not tamed and controlled, it will take over.

What will you do with jealousy? Listen to its blind, vindictive comments as they sear your soul? Be driven to obsession in an angry game of revenge? Or tame it and bring it into submission so that it lies down at your feet and does nothing but purr?

11

MARY

WHEN GOD SINGLES YOU OUT

Mary sat stunned and silent. "The Messiah," she murmured, "I'm to be the mother of the Messiah?!"

She glanced around the dark room. Her mind was full of questions. *It couldn't have been a dream,* she thought. She put her hands to her face, then gripped the edge of the table. She breathed out and closed her eyes. *Think,* she told herself, *think.*

She pieced together the entire conversation from the moment Gabriel had appeared. She ran his words over and over in her mind. "You will give birth to a son . . . He will be called the Son of the Most High . . . His kingdom will never end . . . The Holy Spirit will come upon you . . . "

She swallowed and breathed deeply again, noticing her heartbeat. It was slowing down now. Her nervousness was disappearing.

Suddenly she gasped. "Joseph! What am I to tell Joseph?"

She bowed her head and tightened her lips. *He'll never believe this, never.*

She stood and walked to the doorway, looking out.

Had anyone heard or seen the angel? How could she explain this to her mother and father, to her friends, to . . .

She tried to imagine Joseph's face. The wedding was still nearly a year away. Of course, he would notice. Her stomach would grow. What would he say? What would he do?

She went to her bed and fell onto it. She told herself to think, to pray, to trust. But her heart was quaking again. *Joseph will divorce me,* she thought. *He's an honorable man. That's what he'll do.*

Mary swallowed and shook her head. "I just didn't think it could ever be me," she murmured.

Suddenly she jumped up. "But how do I know?" she asked out loud. "How can I be sure it *wasn't* a wild dream?"

She thought of her cousin, Elizabeth. *The angel said she was with child, in her sixth month,* she thought. *If all this is true, then she'll know too.*

Moments later her parents walked in the doorway. Her mother exclaimed, "Mary, you've let the fire die."

Mary turned and looked at the coals. "I'm sorry, Mother. I was . . . " she paused and looked away. "Distracted."

"Well, I hope you'll not do this when you and Joseph are married. No man likes a cold house."

Mary nodded her head. "I'm sorry."

She waited. Her father gave her a brief hug and touched her hair. "No matter, Daughter. A man such as Joseph will find joy in your smile. That's enough. I did." He looked at his wife and laughed. "Why, I'll bet your mother has let the fire go out—"

Mary's mother broke in. "Shush, you."

Mary smiled weakly and tried to calm herself. "I've decided to take a journey."

Immediately both parents were looking at her.

"What?" exclaimed her father.

"Just a small journey—to see Elizabeth and Zechariah."

"A small journey?" cried her mother. "That's in Judea, near Jerusalem. You'd be gone for months."

Mary shook her head. "I've made up my mind. I'm betrothed now. I want to see a priest. And who better than Zechariah?"

Mary's father studied her face. "Is something wrong, Daughter?"

She bowed her head, then looked up. "Nothing is wrong. But strange things are happening in our times. Perhaps soon, the Messiah . . . "

"Bless the name of the Lord," said her father quietly.

"Bless His holy name," repeated Mary and her mother.

"It will probably be my last chance to see them for many years. So please, Father, may I go?"

He glanced at his wife. She nodded.

He said, "Levi will take you. I can give him some time off from the shop. He'd like a trip anyway."

"That will be perfect," said Mary.

As she pulled the covers down from her bed later that night, Mary gazed out into the street in front of her house. "Mary, mother of the Messiah," she said out loud. She shivered. "It sounds so preposterous."

She listened to the sounds of the night and touched her stomach. *Has it already happened?* she wondered. She breathed deeply. *When I come back,* she thought, *it will be obvious. What will mother and father say?*

She shivered again and bowed her head. "Please, Lord, help me to trust You."

She fell asleep wondering what Elizabeth would say. You'll find what Elizabeth said in Luke 1:42-45. It was a remarkable revelation and confirmation of Mary's call to be the mother of the Messiah, Jesus Christ. But what does Mary's story have to do with you and me?

Her story is a marvelous picture of a situation which most of us, at one time or another, will face. I'm not talking about being the mother of God; I'm talking about that situation in which God singles us out for some special task. It could be a call to be a missionary, pastor, teacher, or leader in the church; a call to a special ministry—to business people, or housewives, or unwed mothers, or the local jocks; a call to go to a special group, or a special person. Such calls often happen during the high school or college years. You may one day be the recipient of such a call.

WHAT IS A CALL?

But what is a call? Is it some mystical experience where God speaks and you hear, where your life is changed forever in one blinding flash? Or is it some subtle conviction, kneaded into your soul during years of exposure to the Bible, truth, and God's people? Or is it something else, something unexplainable?

Many good, honest, committed Christians have struggled with the nature of God's call to a special task. They've wrestled with "God's will for their lives," expecting that some sudden revelation will settle the issue once and for all. They're certain that when the time comes, God will speak.

Moses met God at the burning bush on Mt. Horeb. Samuel heard a voice in the night. Isaiah was lifted up into the very throne room of heaven. John the Baptist was "filled with the Holy Spirit" from birth. Paul met Jesus on the Damascus Road. So powerful was his revelation that he was blinded for three days.

Could this happen to you? Anything is possible with

God. But there are several facts to consider.

1. God communicates in many different ways. If He chooses to issue a call on your life, He has many means at His disposal.

2. Often, God's call on a person's life is unanticipated. People who are "looking" for a call probably don't need anything dramatic. Their desire is enough.

3. In the cases mentioned earlier, the tasks were so monumental that the people involved could never have imagined their call. Can you imagine a modern Moses looking for a call to lead the people of South Florida to a new land which they'd have to conquer when they got there?

If God wants to call you to a task, He's quite capable of doing everything necessary to communicate it. More than likely, He'd do it by normal means—Scripture, the counsel of others, prayer, and wisdom. We don't need to look for some dramatic moment.

So what is a call? I'd say it's a growing conviction that God wants you to do a certain task. That conviction leads to action. Action results in confirmation. And action and confirmation eventually lead to fruit. A person with a true call on his life will act on it, however it occurred, and will see God work. That work may not be spectacular, but it will produce real disciples, and God's people will be nurtured and blessed.

Let's go back to Mary. What distinctives can we see in her that might have parallels in our lives? I see several principles that can apply to a situation in which a person believes God has singled him or her out for a special task.

TROUBLED?

When Gabriel appeared to Mary (Luke 1:26-38) he greeted her, "Greetings, you who are highly favored! The Lord is with you."

As if the appearance of an angel in her house wasn't enough, Luke comments, "Mary was greatly troubled at his words and wondered what kind of greeting this might be" (Luke 1:29).

Mary was *troubled*. I like that. It's human, isn't it? It reminds us of our frailness. It's one of the first things that happens to anyone who receives a call from God: that person will be troubled. Why? One, because what God asks that person to do won't be ordinary; two, it will probably affect the whole of that person's life; three, it will force that person to set aside personal ambitions and plans; and four, it may be a task that the person finds downright distasteful.

When I received a call to the ministry in January 1973, I felt all of those things. I didn't want to be a minister. The mental impression was so strong when it happened that I immediately began arguing with God out loud. (I was alone in a small church.) At the time, I didn't know exactly what I wanted to do with my life. But one thing was sure: I didn't want to be some lackluster guy in a pulpit boring people for an hour every Sunday. (That was, at the time, my unfortunate view of the pastorate.) At one point I even began crying and saying, "How could you do this to me, Lord?"

I was troubled. Mary was troubled. You'll probably be troubled too. It's a natural human reaction. You needn't be ashamed of it, if that's the way you initially respond. God understands. Even Moses made several attempts to divert God from calling him to go to Egypt (see Exodus 3–4). So you're in good company.

LOGIC!

The second thing we see after Mary's troubled feelings was the relentless power of logic. Gabriel explained in Luke 1:30-33 that Mary would give birth to a son, and that that son would be Jesus, the Messiah. Mary's amazed answer is, "How will this be, since I am a virgin?"

Again, I like her honesty and her logic. She was saying, "There must be some mistake. I'm not even married yet."

It's not that she was looking for a way out; she was simply trying to understand what was going on. It didn't make sense to her. She probably wasn't to be married for a year, and the way Gabriel talked, all this would happen in the next day or so. Perhaps she had a momentary vision of being forced to have sexual relations prematurely, which would have been a horror to a righteous Jewish woman.

What I like even more about this situation is that Gabriel patiently answered her questions. Sometimes I get the impression from Christians that you shouldn't ask God certain questions, like: "Why is there evil, Lord, if You're loving?" "What about the heathen who have never heard about You?" "Why did this tragedy happen to me?" But the Lord is never displeased by questioning Christians. In fact, as I study the Bible, I find that whenever people asked God (and Jesus) questions, they received very forthright and direct answers—no hedging, no ifs, ands, or buts, nothing but straightforward, loving answers.

One thing that will happen to you when you face such an experience is that you will have questions, multitudes of them. Don't be afraid to address any of them to the Lord. He'll answer. Maybe it will be through His Word, or a friend, or a book, or an experience, but He *will* answer. He has obligated Himself. After all, He said to Jeremiah, "Call to Me and I will answer you and tell you great and unsearchable things you do not know" (Jeremiah 33:3).

The Lord isn't in the business of mystifying people.

He invites our questions, no matter how difficult they may appear. And believe me, the one Mary asked was difficult. How *could* a virgin have a baby? Mary knew how babies happened. She had reality rooted in her bones.

Though Mary might not have understood Gabriel's answer in Luke 1:35 ("The Holy Spirit will come upon you, and the power of the Most High will overshadow you"), she did get an answer. Furthermore, Gabriel provided her with some remarkable confirmation: her barren cousin, Elizabeth, had conceived in her old age. It was as though God knew how difficult these facts would be to believe, so He provided a two-stage object lesson. First, a woman beyond childbearing age would conceive a baby by normal means; then a virgin would conceive. It would provide Mary with at least one person who understood.

I found that when I was called to the ministry, I had numerous questions. How would I go about becoming a minister? Should I just walk into the church and announce, "I'm here"? I began firing questions to every Christian I met. Fortunately, they were all patient and helped me on the road to an education and personal growth.

EXPLAINING IT!

There was something behind Mary's question that anyone who receives a call will experience. It's this: how can you explain what has happened to outsiders, especially people who may not share your Christian convictions?

One of the first things that hit me after I sensed a call to the ministry was "What am I going to tell my parents?" Neither of them shared my "born-again" zeal and fundamentalist ideas. But they seemed to be able to accept it, so long as it didn't affect family life too much. But going into the ministry was something else. I was terrified at the thought of having to go home and tell my parents.

Similarly, imagine Mary's plight. Telling someone you want to be a minister is one thing, but imagine having to tell someone that the baby you are carrying is of the Holy Spirit? If both Mary and Joseph found the idea hard to accept, what about those who didn't have angelic appearances or visions? This is probably the hardest element of a call. It's something so personal that it often defies explanation.

CONFIRMATION

God will not leave you without friends and help. Gabriel immediately gave Mary her cousin, Elizabeth, to confirm her "call." After Mary had traveled to see her, Elizabeth's first words must have been balm to Mary's soul. She cried out, "Blessed are you among women, and blessed is the child you will bear! But why am I so favored, that the mother of my Lord should come to me? As soon as the sound of your greeting reached my ears, the baby in my womb leaped for joy. Blessed is she who has believed that what the Lord has said to her will be accomplished!" (Luke 1:42-45)

Mary had found a friend, a kindred spirit, one who knew and understood the things that few would understand in her lifetime.

Similarly, the Lord will provide you with external affirmation that He has called you to a task. It may be through the encouragement and counsel of others, or seeing results from your efforts. But it will be something *objective*, not just something within yourself.

Mary must have wondered about the strange circumstances that had plummeted into her life. However "saintly" we make her, she was all human. She questioned. She mulled things over. Luke says later, when Jesus went into the temple as a boy and stunned the elders with his questions and answers, that Mary "treasured all these things in her heart" (Luke 2:51). Although the Lord's choice of Mary as the mother of Jesus was an act of grace, God never makes such choices lightly. He saw in her a combination of faithfulness, reverence, obedience, and commitment that set her above others. But like anyone else, she needed reassurance. God gave it to her through Elizabeth, and then later through Joseph. The things she would face, the gossip that would be directed at her, all the rumors and lies that people would start, could easily crush her spirit. She would need people to help her remain faithful.

That to me is one of the marvels of walking with Jesus Christ. He never asks us to be anything more than human. He understands our fears, our doubts, our worries. He knows what it's like to be the object of hatred, rumor, and slander. It's easy to freeze up, give in, even run in the face of such things. So He gives us a few friends who will keep telling us the truth and reminding us that God is with us.

SUBMISSION

The fifth element of receiving a call is submission. Will you obey the Lord? Will you do as He asks?

It's surprising how many Christians fight the Lord about such things. They pull out their excuses and offer their rationalizations, but none of it makes sense. God wants to give us His greatest blessing, but we often treat it as a curse.

Not Mary. Once she'd gotten the answers she needed, she bowed at the Lord's feet. "I am the Lord's servant . . . May it be to me as you have said" (Luke 1:38). It's that submissive, eager spirit that I think made the Lord choose Mary. After all, this was an irrevocable decision. When you go into the ministry or start a work for God, you can always change course, make modifications, or even call it quits. But Mary was to have a baby. That child would impact her entire life. Once she conceived, there was no going back, no wavering.

Think of it. She was embarking on a course that called for the highest level of responsibility and commitment: mothering the Son of God! Moreover, for many years it would look like she'd sinned. Only Joseph, Elizabeth, and perhaps a few others would know what had really happened. And finally, imagine her own sense of inferiority in the face of raising Jesus—God Incarnate! But she accepted it all. "Whatever you say, I will do, Lord!" Can you approach the will of God like that?

JOY

What then was the end result of Mary's commission? Joy. She rejoiced and exalted God.

Luke 1:46-55 records the famous prayer of Mary which we call "The Magnificat." It is so named because the Latin translation begins with the word, "magnificat," which means "My soul magnifies or exalts God." In other words, "My whole being can no longer hold it in. I have to shout out how great the Lord is!" It all came in a rush. Her words are, in fact, a series of linked quotations from Hannah's prayer in 1 Samuel 2:1-10 (when God gave her a son) and from other places in the Psalms. It's quite clear that Mary knew her Bible (another indication of why God may have chosen her). She exploded with joy and praise once everything came together.

What is even more beautiful is her humility. Her words in Luke 1:48-49 demonstrate her sense of unworthiness. Her heart exalted because God had chosen her. It was unbelievable. "How could God choose me? Why? It's too amazing to be true. And yet it *is* true!"

Have you ever met anyone who thought he was "God's gift to the world"? There are a lot of people like that carousing about these days. They're not amazed that God might have chosen them for some ministry or task. Their only amazement is that God didn't do it sooner! They're the type of people who are still looking for a vacancy in the Trinity.

But Mary demonstrates an attitude far removed from that kind of pride. She recognized immediately that this was a gift from God. Being chosen is a gift. It should breed humility, not haughtiness.

Sometimes we don't notice all the little ways that we exhibit pride—through name-dropping, patting ourselves on the back, telling about our exploits, and so on. It's all a game. "Be somebody!" "Let people know you're important."

And then there's Mary, this humble little girl from Nazareth. All she could think to respond was, "Thank you, Lord. I know I'm not worthy. But I'm so overwhelmed to be included in Your plan. How can I thank You enough?"

If you sense a call from God to do some work in this world, seek that humility that sees it all as grace. A gift. From God to you. From you to others.

That's the only way you'll keep it all in perspective, and find joy in the process.